ONE SMALL PEBBLE . . .

A Thousand Ripples

ONE SMALL PEBBLE . . .
A Thousand Ripples

By Les Gee

朱

10 9 8 7 6 5 4 3 2 1

This book is dedicated to my late parents, who made the seminal decision eight decades ago to endure the unimaginable sacrifices and hardships of immigration so that we who were not even born then would have better destinies. We of all future generations are and will be forever indebted to Allan and Sin Wong Gee.

CONTENTS

One small pebble . . . a thousand ripples.

"Just as ripples spread out when a single pebble is dropped into water, the actions of individuals can have far-reaching effects."

—DALAI LAMA

INTRODUCTION

There is seldom a day that I forget to be grateful for all that my wife, Lila, and I have and can do. Our lifestyle of comfort ("luxury" is a better word, but I avoid boastfulness) results from the confluence of two incredible elements. One is, of course, my parents with their pioneering spirit and courage to utterly uproot themselves from China to immigrate here to America, ignoring the possible challenges and hostilities they might, and did, encounter. The second is America herself, who, like no other country or civilization anywhere and anytime in this world, offered the miraculous and propitious opportunity for my parents to create and build a life beyond recognition from their very humble beginnings.

You see, my father came here from a destitute rural village in Canton, China in 1939 with merely a trunk of clothing and fifty U.S. dollars. After a seven-year separation in opposite hemispheres, having married my mother in Canton in 1937, he was finally able to bring her to America in 1947. With my mother's encouragement and support, my father created the locally famous chain of Sav Mor Liquor Stores in the Bay Area of Northern California.

This successful enterprise not only empowered him to raise the six of us children in comfort (luxury), but with this business he was able to sponsor by employment many other Cantonese families, so that they too could have their chances at the great American dream, most of which efforts were not in vain.

The impetus behind my writing this book is primarily for posterity. It saddens me to think that our children, our grandchildren, and all their progeny might not learn of my parents' humble beginnings. I do not want these descendants—as they purchase their luxury cars, build their beautiful houses, and educate their children at the finest universities—to ever forget these two elements, my parents and America, made it all possible.

Secondly, I am motivated to remind the world that courage and industriousness in a society that is conducive to entrepreneurship and capitalism can synthesize unimaginable success within one mere generation.

My writing endeavor started in the early 2000s, while my father was still alive. (My mother died in 1997.) As his health was beginning to fail, he shared more and more anecdotes of his and my mother's past. I had the wonderful privilege of spending more time with him through his final years, and I realized the need for me to record his and my mother's biographies. This work initially began as a memoir. But as I progressed in my research, I was stymied by the paucity of information in my quest for detailed facts. Many of my parents' contemporaries were either already deceased or were failing in their memories. Ultimately, I realized that I could convey the exact spirit of their story with a biographical novel. Even if I fictionalize the details of specific events and dialogues, I could with integrity tell their story, as long as I adhered to two fundamentals of a biographical novel: One, that I strive to portray the characters with fidelity—none of their behaviors and conversations in my writing are exaggerations beyond what they might have actually done or said. And two, that the historical backdrop of their experiences must remain factually accurate.

The story is told in two distinct chronological segments. Part One is told in third person from my father's perspective. Beginning in Part Two, I shift to narrating in first person as I had come into being at that point (in 1951).

Here begins the odyssey of two people who, whether with deliberate intent or unconsciously out of instinct, fulfilled a shared vision of caring for future generations more than they thought of themselves.

Part One

"The same boiling water that softens the potato hardens the egg. It's about what you're made of, not the circumstances."

—AUTHOR UNKNOWN

LITTLE PEBBLES

The two little boys sat idly at the edge of a large pond that had been left by a recent monsoon. The schoolmaster had fallen ill that afternoon and sent all the children home early. But Suey Fong and his buddy, Soon Goh, knew they each would be punished for playing hooky if they returned to their homes too early.

"Should we go yet?" Soon Goh was impatient.

Suey Fong cautioned, "It's still half an hour before school would have let out. Even then, we must walk slowly since we're already about halfway home."

So, the two continued tossing pebbles into the pond to see who could toss them the highest and still get closest to the center. "Look, the higher I toss it, the bigger the rings . . . even with a small pebble!" observed Suey Fong. Thus, it became a contest of making the biggest ripples with the smallest pebbles.

"You remember what the teacher talked about this morning? I want to go there when I grow up," declared Suey Fong.

"Do you think it's really true there's a mountain made of actual gold?"

"Yes. Of course. He's a teacher and he knows everything. You saw it on the map . . . Gum Shan [Golden Mountain.] It's way across the ocean." Suey Fong waved an arm aimlessly into the distance. "People there are very rich. They can eat chicken drumsticks every day."

Eventually, the sun sank halfway toward the hills. The two boys sauntered back in a serpentine path to their respective homes on the village's main dirt road, which had been turned into an obstacle course by the rain-filled ruts left by the wooden carts the farmers used to drag their produce to market.

Soon Goh's father was a civil servant, and the family lived in a spacious, comfortable house on the hillside of Kee Hing Lee village in the Toisan District of the Canton Province. Suey Fong had been there once to play with Soon Goh, and he was impressed with the abundance of toys and the huge play area in the large home's courtyard. But after that, they were able to play together only at school. Soon Goh's parents did not want their son associating with an orphan farm boy.

Suey Fong lived with his mother in a small earthen brick house at the base of the hill. He never knew his father and was never told much about him except that he had descended from the old and proud Gee clan.

It was about the right time when Suey Fong got home from school, but he received a scolding anyway. Not for leaving school early, but for not gathering enough pig dung the day before. His mother was severe. "How are we going to have enough to eat if you don't bring in enough fertilizer? You will starve us to death!" He was too young to remember much of the last famine, but he did remember going hungry for long periods years back. Having nothing to do with the lack of pig dung, it was one of those many times when torrential floods had washed away entire rice crops. He surely did not want to be the one responsible for bringing starvation upon his mother and himself again. And he was glad to get out of hearing range as he went out into the field, clunking the heavy decrepit wooden bucket and dragging the rusty spade behind.

Frustrated by the scarcity of pig dung this evening, he stood patiently behind a massive water buffalo that was unloading himself of large brown clumps still steaming as they plopped onto the dirt road. Thinking the beast was finally done, Suey Fong eagerly ran up behind him, only to be utterly surprised by an enormous burst of liquidy-brown matter that spattered onto his entire body. Immediately dropping the bucket and spade, he ran along the half-mile trail back to the pond where he and Soon Goh had been earlier, and soaked and scrubbed in the water until he was sure he was completely cleansed of the unpleasant emission. En route, he had also accumulated a layer of mud, having fallen several times from stepping into water-filled potholes left by the hooves of various work animals, including the now deplorable water buffalos.

After returning to and reclaiming his bucket and spade, and scooping up the rest of the remains the water buffalo had abandoned, he was glad to finally head home for supper. But he dawdled and stepped slowly so that his tears would dry up before arriving home. He would not want to chance another scolding if he were to reveal to his mother what had happened. He cried not because of the disgusting event, but because of the humiliation from the people laughing at him as he was desperately rushing along the trail to the pond. At least he encountered fewer people along this trail than he would have had he taken the main road from the village gateway.

Along the way home, he also gathered an armload of kindling and straw so that there would be a surplus of cooking fuel. It would please his mother that he did not have to be asked to do so, especially if she were to find out what had just happened.

That evening, as with many evenings, their meal consisted of a bowl of white rice steamed with bits of dried salt-preserved fish *(hom yee)* and a vegetable from their own yard. This night, the vegetable was boiled bok choy flavored with fermented shrimp paste *(hom ha)*.

After dinner, he found refuge in his schoolbooks. He was glad that a full moon beamed her illuminating brilliance into the room, so that he could study late into the night without a candle.

He could not get Gum Shan out of his mind. Instead of practicing the ten new words that his teacher assigned during the calligraphy lesson, he repeatedly and artistically brushed out the characters for "Gum Shan" with his camel hair brush and ink block.

Lying in bed, he again thought about the humiliating catastrophe with the water buffalo and muttered to himself, "I'm going to grow up and never have to gather animal droppings again. Ever."

A DREAM ACROSS THE VAST PACIFIC

Suey Fong and Soon Goh remained classmates and friends even into their teens although Soon Goh was a few years older. The schools in China at that time, in the 1930s, did not have distinct grade levels by age. (Suey Fong knew his friend as "Soon Goh" because "Soon" was his given name and the suffix "Goh" is how the Chinese respect an older male. The literal translation of "Goh" is older brother.)

On a balmy sunny day, not unlike the day they were tossing pebbles into the pond five years earlier, the two were strolling the rocky south bank of the Pearl River. Every so often, one of them would pick up a stone and try to hurl it as far out into the river as he could. They were now vying for distance. The two could have been brothers sharing much in appearance. They both possessed a high forehead, deeply furrowed when they both squinted in the glaring bright sunlight. Of course, they both possessed the Chinese characteristics of high cheekbones and the noticeably absent nose bridge between their eyes. The only observable difference was their complexion. Suey Fong had a darker olive skin from having spent much more time working outdoors, whereas Soon Goh's family had hired hands to do the outdoor chores.

"You see those ships?" Suey Fong pointed to distant puffs of dark gray steam from the ships down the river. "They're going to Gum Shan. You should go with me. My mother tells me I have an aunt, an uncle, and some cousins there already and that they would put me up until I start earning money. I'm sure they would not mind if you came with me."

"No, I can't, Suey Fong. My parents aren't there. Besides, you can't go either. They are your aunt and uncle there, not your parents. My father works for the government, and he knows the laws there."

In 1882, the United States Congress passed the Chinese Exclusion Act, which sought to curtail Chinese immigration to the United States and forbade the approximately 150,000 already brought there (mostly to complete the California seg ment of the First Transcontinental Railroad) to ever become American citizens or to own property. (Ironically, during these last two decades of the 1800s, the symbolically welcoming Statue of Liberty was being erected in the New York Harbor.) Most of Congress, being comprised entirely of European Americans and having never seen an actual Chinese person before, was easily convinced that the Chinese were culturally unfit to be Americans as they were deemed "unassimilable," a word that was used frequently in political conversations at that time. The Chinese looked different, they dressed differently, and the argument was to either allow the West Coast to "descend into the heathen worship of Confucius or uphold the rightful worship of God." While many of the post–Civil War Republicans resisted these arguments as Southern slaves were being emancipated, the Democrats eventually prevailed with the persuasive claims that cheap Chinese labor was a threat to the unions on the West Coast. (The Democratic Party had always been the "working man's" party.) Thus, this legislation that may have originated with a xenophobic motive was ultimately enacted under the guise of economic justification. This law, followed by numerous extensions upon expiration and fortifications by amendments, was not repealed until 1943.

Suey Fong was not deterred. "They [Immigration and Naturalization Service, INS] don't know that. If my aunt and uncle claim me as a son, and if my cousins call me 'brother,' they must allow me in. I would just have to work hard to pay them back. I promised my mother that I would one day go to Gum Shan, become very rich, and then send for her. We would never live poor again."

In Suey Fong's time, under the then-prevailing version of the Chinese Exclusion Act, only the children of Chinese Americans were permitted to immigrate to the U.S. and reunite with their parents. But due to the destruction of the only available immigration records in the 1906 San Francisco Earthquake and Fire, in conjunction with the fact that China kept no official birth records at all, INS had to essentially accept a sworn affidavit of parenthood in order to allow a child to come to the U.S. from China. And the only means by which the INS could verify such a claim was through rigorous interrogation of both the parents and the alleged children on matters that should be ordinarily known if the claimed parent-child relationship was in fact authentic. Of course, this was the perfect flaw for would-be Chinese Americans to exploit. Someone who aspired to come to America would "buy paper" from a willing Chinese American citizen. That is, the sponsoring "parents" (usually relatives, but sometimes mere friends) would claim the aspirant to be a son, who upon arriving would be indebted to the sponsoring parents for a sum usually calculated at $100 for each year of age. Hence, Suey Fong's paper was $2,000, he being age 20 at the time. ($2,000 in 1939 would inflate to about $30,000 today.) These aspirants came to be known as "paper sons."

Further, it was rare that girls were brought to America in this way. There was an unspoken anti-proliferation motive, revealed in off-record Congressional exchanges, behind this gender limitation in the Chinese Exclusion Act. If America made it even more difficult for girls than boys to immigrate, there would be fewer American-born Chinese, who would then constitutionally have to be recognized as American citizens. But the public explanation for this limitation was the allegation that Chinese women tended to be prostitutes and therefore should not be allowed.

Suey Fong's dream of going to America, even as a paper son, never ebbed from the first time he heard of Gum Shan at the age of ten. Rather, the dream only swelled, like a flickering ember fueled into an obsessive conflagration by wind and kindling. The stories he had heard and the pictures he had seen were the kindling. The homes had electric lights. Cooking was done indoors with a mysterious burning gas. They had piped in water, even hot water. They had flush toilets. There were automobiles. The children didn't have to wait until they started school to own a pair of shoes; in fact, they could have more than one pair of shoes at a time. What a marvelous place! And he didn't care when he eventually realized that there was no such thing as a mountain literally made of gold. By then, he knew the reference to "Gum" [Gold] was figurative. It simply referred to the opportunity and abundance. (The rumors sprouting from the California Gold Rush gave genesis to this literal naming in China, even though it was quickly realized that the gold mines were not accessible to the Chinese.) But for the opportunities, Suey Fong became obsessed with going to America!

"I know it will be a long journey, Soon Goh. But one day I will cross the Pacific Ocean in one of those ships."

THE VOW

It was September 14, 1937. It was a long day full of fanfare and celebration. Despite the protests from many of the village's most vicious gossip merchants, Suey Fong was able to marry Sin Wong. Unlike him from his impoverished means, she was from a family of wealth. Her father had built a successful cane furniture factory while living in Jakarta, which furniture were sold and exported worldwide. She and her family were well traveled throughout Southeast Asia, having lived in Malaya, Singapore, and Jakarta before finally settling in Foo Shan village, neighboring Kee Hing Lee, in Toisan, Canton. Eventually, her father found even more success after closing his Jakarta furniture factory and rebuilding it in Canton. Thus, those in judgment complained that the couple were from "mismatched doors" ('m poi moon hao).

But the village geomancer, imputed with the power of clairvoyance (perhaps due to her being blind) prevailed when she declared the match to be promising of much good luck. And it was also by her authority that she had designated this particular day, and not any other, for the wedding in order to assure good fortune in the marriage.

The customary dowry of homemade cakes had been delivered to Sin Wong's home the day before, and a coin of acceptance was returned to Suey Fong's mother by the same courier who had brought the cakes.

The morning of the wedding started with a long procession, most everyone clad in bright red silk, through the village led by an ornate sedan chair bearing the young bride of fifteen. (Suey Fong was eighteen at the time.) It was an extravagantly decorated sedan, one reserved for the wealthy. The intricately carved wooden frame had just received a fresh coat of shiny red enamel along with two new silk side curtains, each ornately embroidered in iridescent gold thread, one curtain with a dragon and the other with a phoenix, each creature poised midair.

When the bright red-beaded veil was pulled back from her face, Suey Fong was immediately awestruck by Sin Wong's beauty and clear, almost-white porcelain doll complexion. How was he so deserving of a woman of such pulchritude and status? And how would he atone for taking her from the posh comfort of her wealthy family to join his meager and modest household? Most men of the farm, such as Suey Fong, were destined to marry women also of the farm, all of whom had the dark, rugged complexion menaced by the outdoor sun.

The seeds sown by his teacher eight years earlier were now germinating. The two could not remain in China; a better life had to lie ahead in the Golden Mountain.

Suey Fong's determination hardened even more throughout the ceremony as the bride and groom knelt down and made supplications to the spirits of their deceased ancestors and to the gods to bring them health, a prolific brood, and good fortune *(ho sai gai)*. Sin Wong then performed the symbolically dutiful ritual of serving tea with genuflection to each member on Suey Fong's side of the family. Finally, everyone enjoyed an enormous, and also symbolic, nine-course feast of abundance. For the Chinese, the number nine signifies longevity—longevity of both life and marriage.

That evening, Suey Fong made another vow to his new bride. "Sin, I want to take you to America. There is nothing here for us. There will be no future here for our children. I also worry that Japan will not stop with Manchuria. They could one day decide to come down here."

In 1931, the Japanese invaded Manchuria and by 1939 had claimed full control of the entire region. Rumors were whispered about that Japanese spies had already infiltrated Canton disguised as beggars.

"And, most important, Sin, I want to continue providing you all that your parents have accustomed you to.

"I have an Uncle Som and an aunt in a big city called Oakland there, close to San Francisco, and they will adopt me. It will be easy for me to find work there. That's why it's called Gum Shan."

"Do you know English?" Such a question to a husband in that time and culture was regarded as a challenge and considered unbecoming of a wife, and certainly improper on her first day of being married. But, Suey Fong liked her forwardness. Perhaps it is a paradox of human nature to respect and even admire insubordination.

"I've been studying on my own. And, I want to enroll in this English school in Hong Kong."

"When would we go?" Such a question was considered more appropriate for a wife to ask.

"I'm sorry, Sin, but we cannot both go together at first. I must go alone first, get settled, and obtain my American paper [American citizenship.] Then I can legally come back and bring you with me." (Suey Fong had relied on speculations of others and did not realize that American citizenship would be an impossibility at that time.)

"How long will you be gone?"

"I think less than one year. But I promise I will hurry." The distinct sulfuric smell of spent gunpowder from the celebratory firecrackers that started the day still lingered and hung heavy in the evening air.

"I promise."

THE CROSSING

The Pacific Ocean was particularly fierce, and the frigid winds penetrated Suey Fong's clothes, through his skin, and seemingly down to his marrow. This made the dank darkness below decks aboard the SS *President Coolidge,* even in the daytime, seem more hospitable.

The tedium of his two-and-a-half-week steamer journey was punctuated with reflections of what Suey Fong had left behind along with moments of anxious anticipation of what it would be like when he arrived. He had utterly uprooted himself, sacrificing all that was safe and comfortable in Toisan. He had abandoned all vestiges of familiarity. Now his worldly goods consisted of only a trunk of clothing, an English phrasebook he acquired from English school (studying helped assuage the boredom of the voyage), and fifty U.S. Dollars. He also had been given a blurry photograph of his Cousin Dewey. His cousin, he was told, would be waiting for him at the pier in San Francisco after his interrogation on Angel Island, but Suey Fong feared they would not recognize each other. And, of course, he would have to contend with the immigration interrogation on Angel Island.

Suey Fong shared a bunk in third-class steerage near the engine room with two other Cantonese men also hopeful of better destinies. After the first few days at sea, he became accustomed to and no longer noticed the humming and vibrating of the engines accompanied by the sporadic and syncopated snoring of his bunkmates. He no longer even noticed the occasional sudden and loud rumble as the ship throttled to adjust her course in the middle of the night. Some nights he would fall asleep thinking about how his wife, newly pregnant, was getting along living with her mother-in-law. He knew that his mother often could be cantankerous. He wondered if she was carrying a son or a daughter. He worried that he could not keep his promise of returning for her within a year. Other nights, he simply practiced mouthing English words and phrases. He wondered if his English would be intelligible to Americans.

His bunkmates were not at all talkative. Perhaps all three held the same sense of dislodgement from familiarity, the same sense of apprehension about the challenges that lay ahead in this opportunity called America, and the same uncertainty as to when they would see their loved ones again, if ever. But, perhaps conversation was not necessary. All three held that same stoic countenance that already conveyed to each other an unspoken commonality of being paper sons. An occasional polite nod, sometimes with a grin, and a tacit brotherhood was created.

At one point, for several days the seas, completely undisciplined, pitched the vessel wildly, throwing such a tantrum that Suey Fong woke up one of the nights on the floor, soaking in inches of cold water. He sat up and paused for some time before realizing he had been tossed out of his bunk and rain or seawater, or both, had invaded the cabin. It took him awhile to regain consciousness of his whereabouts because he had been dreaming of an actual childhood memory of flood and famine in Kee Hing Lee, when he had gone to bed hungry and was awakened by floodwaters that had entered the house and drenched him where he slept. After he finally emerged from the fog of this dream, he was glad to remind himself of where he was and that there would be an abundant breakfast waiting for him in the galley the next morning. He changed into dry clothing, climbed back onto his bunk, and drifted off, hoping to not have the same dream of his childhood again.

Aside from his many apprehensions, Suey Fong was quite confident that he had more than adequately prepared for his interrogation. Before departing, he had studied the details his uncle and aunt had provided him over several posts, and his wife had drilled him on these details every night. There were over one hundred questions and answers. Of course, he would have to mentally think of his Uncle Som as his father and of all the mundane details that a real son ought to know—"How old were you when your father returned to the United States?" "What does he do for a living?" "How many brothers and how many sisters do you have in America?" "How old is each one?" "How tall is your father?" "What brand cigarettes does he smoke?" All the details had to be well memorized to satisfy the immigration officials at Angel Island. But, he would wait until the last few days of the journey before reviewing the well-crumpled pieces of notepaper he had hidden at the bottom of his trunk. He wanted the "facts" to be fresh upon arrival. He was acutely aware that any mistake could spell immediate deportation. He would not want the humiliation of having to face his wife and the entire village as a deportee.

It was fortunate that he and Uncle Som already shared the same surname, "Gee." Most paper sons had to assume the adopting family's different name, forsaking their own heritage. It was not until late 1955 when the United States passed an amnesty law saying that these paper son families were able to confess to immigration fraud and reclaim their original family names. There was such a huge sense of pride in family lineage that this amnesty law was widely celebrated, and President Eisenhower, who signed the bill, became much beloved among the Chinese Americans. Still, many paper families did not come forth as acute distrust for the American government was promoted by Chinese newspapers reporting that the McCarthyism endeavor was seeking to deport "dishonest Chinese Americans who might be sympathetic to communist China" (China turned communist in 1949). Even today, many of these perhaps overly cautious families continue to use their paper names.

One early morning after more than two long weeks at sea, the droning of the engines was drowned out by cheers and cries from the deck. "Land! America!" Suey Fong and his bunkmates, all barely conscious, stumbled up to the deck to join the commotion. Suey Fong, still barefoot and not even noticing the hostile coldness of the foggy San Francisco coast, squinted. He looked almost directly into the faint and distant rising sun. Backlit by this brilliant crimson disk emerging from behind the hills, both sun and hill muted only by the dense bay fog, there it was! The Golden Gate Bridge! Splendid and magnificent, just like the pictures he had seen! But this time it was not just a fuzzy black-and-white photograph before him. He was not an outwardly emotional person, but in an instant, he was overwhelmed. Warm tears effusively rolled down his cold, tender cheeks. Thousands of fleeting sparkles magnified through the filter of his tears and danced over the shimmering silvery San Francisco Bay waters. Then he turned and took a glance back down the starboard side beyond the stern and saw nothing but the majestic expanse of the Pacific Ocean rising to a mere horizon. Kee Hing Lee was now nowhere to be seen.

THE ISLAND

As the SS *President Coolidge* lumbered her way under the bridge, Suey Fong compactly crumpled the several sheets of notes into tight balls and dropped them over the stern railing and into the bay as his uncle had instructed him to do. He was relieved to see the paper wads churn and disappear into the white foamy wake. He would be immediately deported if the INS were to discover that he had merely rehearsed a subterfuge to enter America.

It was those instances of discovery (leading to deportation) upon which institutionalized anti-Chinese sentiment was recently buttressed; the INS on the frequent uncovering of immigration fraud confirmed publicly that "the Chinaman brings to this country dishonesty and moral turpitude."

When a human who is fundamentally honest seeks to circumvent arbitrary laws that prevent him from seeking for his family that which immutable nature and instinctual drive ordain him to provide, do we characterize such violations of law as immoral? Victor Hugo in *Les Misérables* built his story on this very question where his protagonist, Jean Valjean, was prosecuted for stealing bread for his hungry and dying niece. Was it the committal of immigration fraud that was immoral or was it the Chinese Exclusion Act that was immoral?

Suey Fong had hours to scan the San Francisco skyline before the steamer docked. The silhouette of the waves of hills randomly sprinkled with clusters of gigantic concrete buildings matched his memory of the pictures he had seen of Gum Shan. Ribbons of golden brown undulated through the hillsides. But, he knew it was merely dry grass, not gold as he might have imagined were it ten years ago.

The cold bay breeze sharply chafing his face was nevertheless exhilarating, and the smell of sea salt hung so thick in the air that he tasted it in his mouth.

Still with his English phrasebook tucked tightly under his left arm as if it were his precious entrée to his American dream, his right arm dragged his small trunk behind him as he unceremoniously set foot onto American land. His hope of hospitality was abruptly dashed by an imposing Caucasian man in green uniform austerely growling, "Down to the ferry! Down to the ferry!" using his large hand to physically divert him, and all other Chinese passengers, in a different direction than everyone else. Suey Fong remembered being warned about the *luhk yee* [green clothes]. They were the government officials of the INS. They were to be feared and respected. Today, the Chinese Americans still use the term *"luhk yee,"* although it is now generalized to refer to any uniformed law enforcement officer.

Another *luhk yee* on the other side of the pier escorted the small group of Chinese men onto a ferry that would take them to Angel Island. This was where they would be interrogated to determine the authenticity of their claimed relations with "parents" in America. This was potentially a literal "do or die" test as many who failed the interrogation would commit suicide rather than face the humiliation of deportation. Some deportees hanged themselves on Angel Island before being deported while others reportedly jumped overboard on the return trip. (Although there has been no evidence, stories were told that certain deportees who were uncooperative or who were being deported for carrying suspected diseases were actually thrown overboard by the Caucasian crew members who then reported the incidents as suicides.) Everyone knew there was the element of risk; estimates run as high as thirty percent failure in the interrogation, resulting in deportation and potential legal consequences for the sponsors. Nevertheless, Suey Fong was confident of his knowledge and was bolstered by his ability to speak some semblance of English.

Upon disembarking on the island, everyone was required to leave his belongings in a holding shed near the administration building. Suey Fong was instantly glad he had disposed of his notes as he correctly anticipated that they would inspect the contents of everyone's luggage. The *luhk yee* in charge of the shed grabbed Suey Fong's English phrasebook and paged through it thoroughly. Satisfied that it contained no cheat notes for his interrogation, the *luhk yee* threw it back at Suey Fong's feet. Suey Fong knew better than to react. Instead, he bent over to pick up his book and forced a nod and a smile. Oddly, the *luhk yee* smiled back.

The small group of new arrivals were shown to the dormitory, simply a large wooden barrack up a steep hill from the administration building with several large rooms filled with metal frame bunks two or three high. Each narrow bunk was supplied with a pillow and a small blanket, but often no mattress because INS indicated that the Chinese did not use mattresses. The bunks were so crowded together that there was just enough walking space for one person at a time to access his bunk. One of the smaller rooms on the second level was reserved for the women as there were much fewer women than men.

There was a large game room, also on the second level, for the men where there was a ping pong table and game tables set up for various Chinese board games such as checkers, mahjongg, and xiangqi (Chinese chess).

The new arrivals were escorted to the game room where a Chinese *luhk yee* spoke to them in Cantonese. "You may be detained here for days and even weeks as government administration works very slowly. You will be examined to be sure you are not bringing any diseases to America. Additionally, it will take time for your respective American relatives to be interrogated to corroborate your answers. Meals will be served three times a day in the mess hall down by the administration building. If you brought money with you, you can purchase American food in the cafeteria behind the mess hall." Suey Fong thus surmised that the mess hall would be serving Chinese food.

He found the Chinese food to be not very tasty and usually cold. But this was not much different than the food he received on the steamer. Realizing he had only fifty precious dollars, he never ventured to try a sandwich or a Coca Cola there. Some of his bunkmates spoke of the novelty of completely new tastes in American food, and he often caught a whiff of some of the aromas that wandered into the mess hall. He, nevertheless, dismissed the curiosity and resisted temptation.

The days of waiting in the locked dormitory were no more interesting than the two and a half weeks of monotony at sea until one of his bunkmates brought back a violin from the storage shed. The men were allowed to fetch and return items from their luggage twice a day. Suey Fong had learned to play the violin in school well enough that he was teaching the owner of this violin some classical Chinese opera tunes.

Suey Fong thus became a source of entertainment for the dormitory. The large airy game room with its cold hard floor and high ceiling created a basilica-like echo enhancing the sweet sadness of the violin's mournful wailing. It was reported back to Suey Fong that the reverberations pierced the thin wall into the women's dormitory and that the familiar tunes of cathartic Chinese opera induced many tears—perhaps it was the combination of the sense of imprisonment along with the tunes conjuring memories of the many familiar tragic tales related in classical Chinese opera.

In the evenings, Suey Fong stayed up in the game room writing letters back to his bride. He was appreciative that there was electric lighting. Back in Kee Hing Lee, he could only write at night whenever there was a full moon. His odyssey was just beginning, and he already had much to share. He had sent several letters but realized that it could be a long time before he would see any replies since he had given Uncle Som's address as the return address. He could only hope that she and his mother were getting along well.

Laying in his bunk, he would reminisce about the last dinner before he left. His bride squeezed in a few more practice quiz questions for his interrogation throughout the evening, and his mother made sure it was an extra-special dinner. She and Sin Wong had slaughtered, feathered, and roasted their finest chicken from the yard. Suey Fong was given both chicken drumsticks, a special and appropriate honor, but he only ate one of them giving the other one to his bride. "You are carrying our baby. You should have more nourishment."

"No, but you must be healthy for the long journey."

In the end, the two took turns reducing the chicken leg to its bare bone, after which time Sin Wong suddenly broke into tears.

"Sin, please don't. Please don't. It will only be a year. Maybe sooner."

"Not soon enough to see your baby born."

"We'll see. We'll see. But, tears are bad luck at the dinner table. So please don't cry, Sin."

The two had not noticed that his mother had left the table during the chicken drumstick exchange until she returned clutching a black quilted silk vest. "Suey Fong, this is the only thing I ever had left of your father's. This is yours now, and I want you to keep this with you all the time."

In anticipation of his interrogation interview, Suey Fong had taken his American-style business suit from his trunk and laid it neatly at the foot of his bunk, smoothing the two pieces by hand each night hoping to expunge the two and a half weeks' accumulation of wrinkles. And beneath the suit, he had also unfurled his father's silk vest planning to wear that also. He was able to acquire this dark brown secondhand suit in China in exchange for several bundles of Chinese broccoli *(gai lan)* from their garden. His uncle had advised him that if he dressed more western, he may be treated more favorably by the immigration officials.

THE INTERROGATION

Compared to many other bunkmates, Suey Fong was fortunate to be called to his interrogation quickly. He had heard that in the past some of them had been held for as long as one or even two years. The third week there, the same Chinese *luhk yee* who had given him orientation came to escort him to the administration building. He was excited to put on his suit and look American. The suit was much too large for his slight size, even with the quilted vest underneath his coat, but he was nevertheless proud to look American.

The *luhk yee* sent him to the toilet before leaving the barrack; he warned Suey Fong that the interview could last a long time, and the interrogators are very reluctant to allow toilet breaks, being suspicious that the interviewees would excuse themselves only to view cheat notes that could have been secreted in their clothing.

In the context of the impending interrogation, this simple trip to the toilet was suddenly like none before. As he walked onto the cold hard tile, the bathroom took on an eerie, lugubrious atmosphere as he suddenly recalled witnessing a most ghastly sight the second day he was there. He became queasy walking past the very point where he had seen a completely limp corpse suspended from the overhead pipes with knotted up pillowcases around its neck. Pinned to its black Chinese style robe was a notice, "Entry denied." The man had hanged himself.

On their way to the administration building, Suey Fong boasted that he could speak English, but then the *luhk yee* admonished, "Let me speak for you. You must speak only Chinese, and you must only speak directly with me. I will translate." Suey Fong understood the gravity of this interview.

Suey Fong was shown a solitary metal chair on one side of a large army green-metal table. The Chinese *luhk yee* took one of three upholstered chairs at the opposite side. In a moment, three stolid Caucasian *luhk yees* in their austere green uniforms entered the room and robotically removed their caps; two of them took the remaining seats at the table. The third one sat at a small table equipped with a typewriter. The Chinese and two of the Caucasian *luhk yees* whispered among themselves, but what was said was completely imperceptible to Suey Fong.

It was a drawn-out interrogation. The typewriter clattered away loudly and conspicuously at first, but eventually the monotonous sound faded into the background. There were more silent moments than dialogue moments throughout the five hours. And, Suey Fong was more intimidated by these long pauses than the moments of actual questioning. During these pauses, the older officer would shuffle, page through, and read silently from a thin stack of notes the typist handed over occasionally. The older *luhk yee* would stop to write in the margins and then whisper with the other two.

And in these long pauses, the vacuum of silence drew back into Suey Fong's mind the vivid sights and sounds of the commotion that ensued the suicide two weeks earlier. Suey Fong would squint and squirm, trying to chase the image of the hanging body away from his mind. But, the harder he tried, the more the morbid image haunted him. The lifeless cadaver—with its limbs completely limp, its dark catatonic eyes still wide open against the pastel skin, its mouth gaping open as if in astonishment, and its head bent at an unnatural angle—swayed back and forth like a pendulum. But, what may have frightened him more were those two terrifying words pinned to the cloak. He knew enough English to read "Entry denied."

The stoic looks on the officers' faces, unchanging as if they were photographs, gave no hint to Suey Fong how the interrogation was progressing. The Chinese *luhk yee* held the same fixed, expressionless look throughout.

It was actually a relief to Suey Fong when every now and then the older officer spoke out loud in English to the Chinese *luhk yee*. The younger officer never addressed Suey Fong the entire time but only held whispered conferences with the older officer and the Chinese *luhk yee*. Suey Fong understood most of the questions, but waited for the *luhk yee* to repeat them in Chinese before responding, also in Chinese, as he had been coached.

At some point, Suey Fong finally heard enough to surmise that an interview had already been conducted with his relatives in Oakland and was comforted when he heard the words "Oakland," "okay," and "very good" as the officer continued to peruse the typed pages.

Finally, the officer evened the bottom edges of the sheets by bouncing them loudly several times on the tabletop, slipped them back into a file folder, and handed the folder to the younger officer. As if on cue, all three stood up at once, each still looking blank, and the older officer announced to the Chinese *luhk yee*, "We'll get back with you tomorrow sometime."

Suey Fong was relieved not only because this interview was over, but almost as much because he was finally able to separate himself from the torturously hard chair after five hours.

Suey Fong spent nearly the entire night sleepless, replaying over and over the questions and answers in his mind, each time trying to make certain to himself that he had not slipped on any of his answers. And he remembered that some of the questions had been asked several times and he needed to assure himself that he had answered it the same way each time.

"Are you married?"

"No."

"Have you ever lived anywhere besides Kee Hing Lee?"

"No."

"Where will you be living?"

"In Oakland."

"Who will be living with you?"

"My father, my mother, two sisters, and a brother."

"What is your wife's name?"

"I am not married."

"What languages do you speak?"

"Only Chinese."

"Who did the cooking when you were in China?"

"My mother."

"Did your wife do any cooking?"

"I am not married." (Married men were not allowed into the United States, lest they might expect to bring their wives. Being married would be cause for immediate deportation.)

Suey Fong also reminded himself that he would probably be called back more times as he noted had been the case with many of his bunkmates. All in all, he felt confident that he had done well, but he still never closed his eyes. Not until the reddish glow of dawn gradually crept through the windows did he sense any exhaustion, mental or physical.

Just as he finally began to succumb to tiredness and start drifting off, he heard keys rattling outside and then a loud metallic click. Then he heard the familiar morning sound of the wooden bar being removed from outside the door. Rapid footsteps thudded louder and louder, announcing some sense of urgency. The Chinese *luhk yee* appeared at the side of Suey Fong's bunk.

"Suey Fong, I just spoke with your interviewer. I have some very good news for you."

SALTINES, AN AUTOMOBILE, AND THE BAY BRIDGE

Suey Fong sat on his trunk in the drafty and cavernous warehouse of the San Francisco pier, waiting patiently and keeping occupied by practicing counting in English the high stacks of shipping containers. He had lately become accustomed to long waits. But his stomach growled impatiently. He had not remembered being so hungry since the last famine in China. He was so excited that morning and didn't want to miss the ferry off Angel Island that he only had half a bowl of cold tasteless congee, a Chinese rice porridge, at breakfast.

As he waited, a Chinese man approached him and uttered something in English so rapidly that Suey Fong did not understand him. The stranger switched to speaking Chinese. Comforted that he was speaking the same familiar dialect of Toisan Cantonese, Suey Fong ventured, "You are Dewey, are you?"

"No. Are you waiting for someone named Dewey?"

"Yes. He must be late," surmised Suey Fong.

"What is your name?"

"Suey Fong."

"Suey Fong, my name is William Wong. While you are waiting for Dewey, can I borrow twenty dollars? I'll bring it right back in a moment."

Suey Fong without questioning, stood up, opened his trunk, reached in and produced two ten-dollar bills and without hesitation handed them to the stranger.

The stranger vanished as quickly as he had shown up without even a thank you.

Perhaps due to miscommunication, it was not until very late afternoon before his cousin Dewey showed up at the warehouse. By then, Suey Fong was as happy to see a box of Saltines tucked under Dewey's arm as he was to see Dewey himself.

"You are Dewey, are you?"

"Yes, Suey Fong, I'm glad to finally meet you. Is this all you have?" Dewey pointed to the small trunk.

"Yes. I don't own very much."

"Okay, let's go to my car parked outside."

"Wait. I have to wait for William."

"Who's William?"

"You don't know William Wong?"

"No, why do we need to wait for him?"

"He just borrowed twenty dollars from me, and he's bringing it right back."

"No. That's probably not his real name, and he's not coming back. You just lost twenty dollars. These people wait around the pier, looking for newcomers just like you. You're no longer in Toisan. You will never see him again . . . or your twenty dollars."

It was all so new to Suey Fong. He had never ridden inside an automobile before. He intently studied the dashboard as Dewey busily juggled three pedals with two feet and manipulated the steering wheel and a lever that projected from the steering column with his hands. He was amazed, amused, and confused as he tried to correlate his cousin's actions with the automobile's movement. But, determined, he thought to himself, "I need to learn how to do this because one of these days, I will own one of these."

"This isn't the Golden Gate Bridge, is it, Dewey?"

"No, this is the Bay Bridge. This will take us to Oakland."

Suey Fong, with mouth gaping in amazement, marveled at this gigantic assemblage of steel cables neatly choreographed to pass the car's side window, dancing up to the top of skyward-towering iron monuments and back down again. Just a few weeks before, he was in awe of the mere sight of the Golden Gate Bridge. Now he was actually traveling on such a bridge.

"I'm told you did very well on your interrogation."

"I'm glad I studied too much. The interrogator kept me a long time and asked many detailed questions and then let me go back to my bunk. I think they were trying to trick me. And, I thought he would call me back for more questioning, but the next day the Chinese *luhk yee* came and told me the interrogator liked me and that I could leave to join my family. Many of my bunkmates were called back repeatedly over many days. Some of them told me they had been there for months. And, some were sent back to China."

"You were lucky to get a good interrogator. Do you have an American name yet? You should have one."

Suey Fong suddenly remembered the nameplate on the desk of the last *luhk yee* he had to sit with after his congee breakfast on the island. Before boarding the ferry, the Chinese *luhk yee* took him to the administrative office to affix his signature to the stack of typed papers from his interrogation. He immediately recognized this *luhk yee* as the one who checked out his English phrase book when he arrived on the island. They exchanged smiles in recognition. Gripping the pen perfectly vertical as if it were a calligraphy brush, he slowly started the first stroke when his hand started trembling.

The Chinese *luhk yee* assured him in Chinese, "It's OK, Suey Fong. It's just routine, and this man likes you." Turning to the Caucasian *luhk yee,* he offered in English, "Mr. Gee is just very excited this morning."

"That's fine. Tell him to take his time."

Eventually, Suey Fong was able to calm down and carefully affix in Chinese characters "Gee Suey Fong."

Again exchanging smiles with the *luhk yee*, Suey Fong braved his English, "Deng you vely much."

"You're welcome. And good luck."

Rising from the desk, Suey Fong noted the first name on the name plate "Allan."

Suey Fong and Dewey had been conversing in Cantonese up to this point, but Suey Fong ventured to try his English on his cousin for the first time. "My name 'Allan.'" A brief tutoring ensued; Chinese grammar does not utilize an equivalent of "to be," but he was willing to adopt the seeming superfluity of "My name *is* Allan." He remembered being confused by the same excessiveness when he was studying English in Hong Kong.

In afterthought, Suey Fong was glad to have adopted the name "Allan," the only Caucasian on Angel Island who ever smiled at him.

A NEW WORLD

Allan thumped his trunk up several steps into his new home and immediately became oblivious to the playfully noisy family members surrounding him when he spotted two light blue envelopes on a table. They each had the familiar dark blue and red hashes along the perimeters signifying Air Mail. They were addressed to him with Canton postmarks. He immediately knew they were from his bride, and in an instant, all the dark and even macabre thoughts and worries that had abused his imagination while on the steamer and Angel Island were vanquished into absurd impossibilities.

He missed her; she missed him. But, at least now they each knew the other was safe.

He was elated to also learn that they had a new daughter, Gee So Jing. In China, the family name always appears first and the given first name [Jing] is placed last. The middle name

[So] is not actually a name but always precedes the first name to designate the generation level in the family. Thus, all future girls born in Allan's family would be preceded by "So." All boys of the same generation would share another common "middle name." One might guess from the sequence of a full name that familial and then generational identification take on greater importance than the individual family member.

So Jing was a robust and healthy baby, and Allan's mother had been a tremendous help to Sin Wong according to the letters. Evidently, the two were getting along well, much to Allan's relief.

The Japanese, Sin Wong reported, had indeed come into Canton. But she reassured him that they were only after the Chinese military and that civilians were not being disturbed. As she was sparse with any details, Allan concluded the Japanese incursion was not consequential.

Allan was astounded by his new home. He had dropped into a new and entirely different universe. In this Oakland Chinatown house at 115 8th Street near Alice Street, he discovered a separate indoor room containing a flushing toilet! (He thought flushing toilets were a luxury only found on steamers and other public places, such as the barracks on Angel Island.) In the same room were a washbasin and an enormous bathing tub, each with knobs that created running water—hot or cold by choice! There was a hole at the bottom of each where the spent water dizzily cycloned away into oblivion! He had to be instructed to close and lock the door before using this room. The house had another room, also indoors, where all the cooking was done—and on a stove that didn't require wood and kindling! Next to it was a large white metal cabinet that hummed, especially loudly in the nighttime, and kept food cold!

But what amazed him as much, and more importantly, comforted him, was his newly adopted family. Having endured frequent and varying degrees of rudeness, sometimes to the point of humiliation, since leaving Canton, he was glad to find himself enshrouded in the warmth and hospitality of his new family.

Quong, the only boy, Lily, and Flora, his three new siblings, were instructed by Uncle Som to respect Allan by addressing him as "Ah Goh," older brother. Allan protested despite his seniority. "You are all smarter than I. You were all born here and can speak English."

"We will teach you," Lily proffered.

Every now and then, one of the cousins would stop and apologize to Allan for speaking English amongst themselves. But he immediately replied that he wanted to hear more English, so that he could become better at it.

The first evening easily crept beyond midnight as Allan and his three cousins traded stories until the parents chased them all off to bed.

The next morning, Flora noticed from inside that Allan had circumnavigated the house three times. So she proceeded outside to ask, "Allan, did you lose something? I can help you find it."

"No. I was just wondering when we flush the toilet and drain the washtub, isn't there a dugout trough somewhere out here to drain everything away?"

"Oh, no, Allan," Flora chuckled. "There are big pipes that run under the house all the way to the street. And then there are bigger pipes underneath the street that collect everyone's wastewater and take it all far, far away."

Allan was delighted and amazed.

FROM BUSBOY TO WAITER

Later the morning of his second day in Oakland, Lily accompanied Allan, teaching him how to ride the Key System Rail into East Oakland. The parents had arranged a job for him as a busboy at a friend's Chinese restaurant, House of Lee. House of Lee was a successful high-end Chinese restaurant that thrived in the same location on Fruitvale Avenue near Foothill Boulevard until the late 1960's. This restaurant, like most Chinese restaurants outside of Chinese neighborhoods, was primarily patronized by, and therefore catered to, Caucasians.

Allan was somewhat puzzled, mildly amused, and necessarily curious to learn of an entirely foreign genre of Chinese food. Chop Suey, Egg Foo Yong, and Fried Ravioli (fried wonton) appeared on the menu. Who in China had ever heard of such dishes? Most of the ingredients (bean sprouts, ground pork, water chestnuts, black mushroom, etc.) were certainly familiar to him. But the methods of preparation and the flavorings bore no resemblance to the cooking he grew up with in China. This restaurant used sauces and flavorings that were mostly sweet and aromatic, whereas he had been accustomed to savory and pungent flavors (such as *dou see* [fermented black soy bean] and shrimp paste.) Indeed, he realized he was discovering a whole new cuisine—Chinese America food. Even more baffling to him, the customers consumed these dishes with knife and fork. He was pleased that occasionally a Caucasian customer would ask for chopsticks.

"Water. Please!" a customer barked.

Allan nudged the waiter standing next to him speaking in Cantonese, "I think Table 14 is calling for you."

"No, he wants *water*. Not *waiter*."

Embarrassed, Allan immediately grabbed the water pitcher and rushed over to Table 14 sloshing water as he ran. "So sorry. I not hear you first time. So sorry!" He dipped his head several times in a bow.

"No worries. You're new here, are you?" The Caucasian gentlemen squinted at the name tag. "Allan? You're doing a fine job. Thank you. My name is Ed, and this is my wife, Grace." Ed presented a benign grin and reached out for a handshake.

Allan put his pitcher down, wiped his right hand dry, extended it and felt the warm welcome from a Caucasian for the first time. "Thank you, sir. Thank you, Ed. Nice I meet you, Grace." He dipped his head again.

"Oh, you're in America. No need to bow."

"Okay." But, he bowed again in acknowledgement. All three exploded in laughter. It would be years before he broke the bowing habit.

In due time, he realized that only few Caucasians displayed the hostility he had experienced aboard the steamer and on Angel Island. He became familiar by name with many of the regular customers who engaged him in conversation. He enjoyed this, as he knew this was improving his English vastly. Within the first year, he had become a waiter, proudly graduating from his brown smock to a tailored black two-piece suit, white shirt, and a red bow tie. And his familiar customers would often specify "Allan's table" on their reservations.

Mr. Lee, the owner, also took an immediate liking to Allan. "You're a hard worker and customers seem to like you. They especially enjoy taking chopstick lessons from you. But, I need you to go to school on your days off to improve your English. One day, I want to see you own a business, too. But you must bring your family home first."

This last sentence struck Allan. He was now to think of America as home, not China as home any longer. And, he should bring his family *home to America*. China was his motherland, but America was now his home.

LETTER FROM SIN WONG

12 February 1939

Dearest Suey Fong [Allan],

I hope you are doing fine in America. We are waiting for you to come home to bring us to Gum Shan.

We are now okay, so I will tell you what has happened. I did not want to tell you too much while the Japanese had been so troublesome, so that you would not worry. I know you have too much else to worry about anyhow.

We are now safe back in our home. But we had to leave for a few months when they [the Japanese] raided our village. It was a long and difficult journey with our daughter So Jing much of the time on my back. Your mother carried as much of our possessions as she could. Hundreds of us were escorted on foot to a camp about 20 Li's [about 7 miles] from home. The camp was run by American nuns who were very kind to us. Many of them spoke Chinese. And, they fed us, gave us clothing, and warm blankets. We should be grateful for the kindness of the Americans.

But I was sad to see that some families were broken up, going to different camps because of the amount of panic and confusion when the Japanese planes flew overhead very close to the ground at the same time that soldiers were marching into the streets of the village. It broke my heart to see two little children, a boy and a girl, alone in the street crying, "Ma Ma! Ba Ba!" I hope they were eventually reunited with their parents.

When we returned home, I found that many things, especially furniture, were gone. But the jade and gold jewelry that I had hidden under some rocks outside were untouched. Other people's homes were completely destroyed by the Japanese bombs.

Please don't worry about us. We are now safely back home.

Write me and let me know when you will be coming back. I miss you very much.

Sin Wong

On October 12, 1938, the Japanese navy landed at Bias Bay, east of Canton. In anticipation of a land invasion, the International Red Cross set up six refugee camps in the outskirts of town and began evacuation of Cantonese civilians into these camps. Indeed, amid the evacuations, the Japanese launched air strikes followed by pillaging of the villages. Canton was ultimately completely purged of the Chinese military. Although the Japanese were in full control of Canton, they were to leave civilians untouched. Subsequent to the infamous "Rape of Nanking" in December of 1937 where civilians—men, women, and even children—were slaughtered and many Chinese women were taken as sex slaves for the Japanese soldiers, Emperor Hirohito did not want to again face the previous vociferous international condemnation and issued an unequivocal order to his top brass to punish any soldier who mistreated civilians in Canton. There were, nevertheless, many civilian deaths dismissed as "collateral damage" and, as well, violations contrary to Hirohito's orders. It was not until February of 1939 that the Cantonese began gradually drifting back home.

After this last letter, the Japanese cut off all communications with America, since China had formally allied with the U.S. against Japan. This was the one precious letter that Allan carefully preserved in a glassine envelope and carried with him everywhere he went. At nights, he would take it out and read it over and over until he eventually remembered it verbatim.

One year to the day since Allan left China, he awoke thinking it would be another routine day of taking the Key Rail to work, caring for his dining customers, and then taking the

Key Rail home late in the night. But one thing was different that day—all day he had a cloud of guilt nagging him like a persistent itch. He had let his wife down. It didn't matter how circumstances had evolved. He had made a promise. The Chinese Exclusion Act, although meant to expire ten years from its original enactment in 1882, had actually been extended and even fortified several times since, making it nearly impossible for him to earn his American citizenship in the near future. His aunt and uncle had also warned him that if he left the U.S., the INS would probably not allow him back in again. The Japanese were in full control of Canton's communication with the outside world. Allan had recently sent a number of letters to his wife, but he was not surprised that he never received any replies, knowing of the Japanese muzzling of communications. He couldn't even be sure that any of his letters got to her. He nevertheless felt personally responsible for his vow to bring her, their daughter and his mother to America within a year. He and his bride were still on opposite hemispheres of the globe.

He climbed into bed and pulled out his bride's February 12 letter. He didn't need to read it anymore; he knew it word for word. In the dark loneliness, he clutched the precious letter, pressing it tight to his chest, and in the quiet of the night he heard a teardrop plop onto his pillow. He felt completely helpless.

ELUSIVE HOPE

It was the Day of Infamy. December 7, 1941. Pearl Harbor. Allan arrived at work on what started as an ordinary tranquil Sunday morning to prepare for the usual Sunday after church stampede. Predictably, the lunch crowd stormed the hostess all at about the same time.

But just as suddenly, a man broke through the crowd at the entrance with an explosive scream, "We've been attacked! We've been attacked! The Japanese have bombed us in Hawaii!" The ambient rumbling voices instantly went silent. Silverware stopped tinkling. Glasses stopped clanging. Dishes stopped thudding. Against almost dead silence, he defended, "I just heard the news!"

A voice from the line challenged, "Are you sure you heard right? We're supposed to be in peace talks with those Japs!"

"I'm sure I heard right! It's no joke! The report came right from Honolulu! They confirmed it was in Oahu somewhere!"

The rumbling voices started up again, this time much louder. Mr. Lee, followed by a trail of employees, including Allan, rushed into the kitchen where a Philco radio was kept in the storage area. Everyone anxiously awaited as Mr. Lee plugged the radio in and waited impatiently for filaments in the vacuum tubes to warm up to their radiant orange glow. The squealing and crackling of the radio came to life. Mr. Lee impatiently jockeyed the dial until the static became an intelligible man's voice. Allan listened intently and translated the report into Cantonese for some of his coworkers. Indeed, the Japanese had launched a devastating surprise air and naval attack on Oahu.

Allan spoke in Cantonese, "They've already taken Canton and much of China. Now they want the rest of the world!" Indeed, the Empire of Japan looked eastward and had her ambitions on the entire Pacific. Emperor Hirohito had made a pact with Hitler to not encroach any further west than Manchuria. Thus, as it was learned later, Guam, Wake Island, Midway, and the Philippines were also attacked by Japan.

Mr. Lee had to interrupt the kitchen rumbling, "We have customers waiting. Please go back to work, and I will tell you if anything important develops."

Everyone returned to their posts to notice that the dining room had turned very quiet with only the murmur of whispered conversations. Will they attack San Francisco next? Will they come here to Oakland? What will President Roosevelt do about this? Did they attack Honolulu and kill civilians? Or did they attack our naval installation and kill soldiers?

Rumors and speculations were clarified the following day when President Roosevelt addressed Congress. Only one hour after the deadly and devastating surprise attack on Pearl Harbor, the ambassador from Japan communicated to the United States State Department, expressing that the continued talks of peace and diplomacy were no longer constructive, but giving no mention whatsoever of the early morning attack that killed more than twenty-four hundred American military personnel and sixty-eight civilians. Nineteen American naval ships were damaged, of which three were completely destroyed, including the celebrated USS *Arizona*. Over three hundred American aircrafts were damaged or destroyed. Pearl Harbor had been utterly surprised, and President Roosevelt in a short but cogent speech (the legendary Infamy Speech) to Congress asked for a declaration of war. It was later learned that Midway and Wake Island had also been attacked. The president's request was granted within hours unanimously save for one dissension from a Republican. The outrage had galvanized unity and patriotism in a previously divided America, she having already been embroiled in the Western theater of the war.

Allan's hope for his family reunion slipped away further and faster into the abyss of a futile wish. It had been more than two and a half years since he last heard from Sin Wong. But he still clung to that last letter protected by the glassine envelope in his pocket at all times.

In 1940, Chiang Kai-shek had already requested America's help against imperialistic Japan. The famous General Joseph

"Vinegar Joe" Stilwell, because of his fluency in Chinese, was commissioned by President Roosevelt as Chiang's American chief of staff to build up the military in China. However, it was General Claire Chennault, sent as military advisor to Stilwell, who was instrumental in keeping open the critical "Burmese Hump," the vital artery that brought American and British military supplies from Rangoon, Burma, into China. The original very rudimentary supply road that was hand-built by the Chinese with pick and shovel was under constant Japanese attack. It was also a dangerously winding and narrow road where entire truckloads of supplies and artillery would tumble down steep cliffs and explode. Chennault eventually saw the wisdom of building air strips for cargo planes to replace the primitive and vulnerable road. Commanding the famous Flying Tigers with P-40's to destroy Japanese offenses along the route, Chennault had C-46 cargo planes carrying supplies taking off from Rangoon as frequently as every fifteen minutes at times.

To support this endeavor, the United States Air Force division of the Army in 1942 established the Venice Army Airfield in Venice, Florida to meet the demands of the Flying Tigers. As Chennault was enlisting both American and Chinese pilots on this mission, the U.S. military became very interested in recruiting bilingual Chinese men to serve in the 4500th Army Air Base Unit in Venice, Florida. This Air Service Group was to be the ground support for the Flying Tigers. (At the time, the Air Force was a division of the U.S. Army.)

Whether it was speculation or pure myth fueled by wishful thinking at the time, it had circulated throughout the Chinese communities that the U.S. would grant American citizenship to any immigrant who served in the U.S. military. Factually, this did happen, but not until 1943 in conjunction with passage of the Magnuson Act, which finally repealed the six-decade old Chinese Exclusion Act.

With this wishful glimmer of hope, Allan felt there was nothing more to lose and gambled on the possible golden fleece of American citizenship. In November of 1942, he enlisted to serve in the Air Force division of the U.S. Army and was predictably stationed at the new air base in Venice, Florida.

But in addition, something bigger, something more powerful and nebulous than gaining citizenship, surfaced in his mind. Every time he looked at his precious last letter from his wife, he felt an inexplicable combination of emotions that included helplessness and anger. He felt there was absolutely nothing he could do, being thousands of miles away from his wife, his daughter, and his mother. He was angry at Japan for her aggression into Canton and now on American soil. He had no idea of the fate of his family. Becoming a part of the American fight seemed to quell that combination of emotions.

It was a call to duty.

ASSIMILATION AND THE AIR FORCE

Spartan and completely exposed on the top and the sides to the Floridian elements, the Willys MB jeep bore no resemblance at all to the cloistering, posh automobiles Allan had recently ridden in, save for the steering wheel, the shift lever, and three pedals on the floor. So, he was glad to see some familiarity when he climbed into a driver's seat for the first time in his life.

Presuming that Allan knew how to drive an automobile, Sergeant Pickering had asked Allan to take the jeep out to the airstrip to pick up a visitor. Operating purely from memory, having watched his cousin and uncle whenever they drove, Allan was able to replicate the basic steps. However, he quickly discovered that the jeep had a temperamental balance between accelerator and clutch; otherwise the engine would instantly protest by dying. Fortunately, after uncountable engine stalls on the way out to the airstrip, he became quite proud of himself for negotiating peace between accelerator and clutch by the time he neared the plane that was waiting on the tarmac. It was not until that evening that several fellow privates revealed to him that he had driven Congressman Emory Price from the airstrip. That was fodder for robust laughter sessions throughout the entire barracks when Allan admitted that he had never driven before. Had he known it was an important government official, he would have told Sergeant Pickering that he should not be the one to transport the congressman. But now he was proud and confident he could successfully handle an automobile.

The war was important in transforming the anti-Chinese sentiment in America. Not only did the government realize that the U.S. and China needed each other as allies united against Japan, but also the proliferation of factories that supported the military, directly and indirectly, virtually eliminated unemployment, which thus mitigated much of the animosity from the labor unions toward the Chinese. In fact, in 1943 a congressman was quoted as saying, "If it had not been for December 7, I do not know if we would have ever found out how good they [the Chinese Americans] were."

The American Civil War was a real-world test of the antebellum doublespeak that defied the pure democratic ideals unequivocally espoused in the ingeniously crafted U.S. Constitution. Now, once again, another war illuminated and defeated a similar political hypocrisy, this time with the Chinese. And again, the U.S. Constitution prevailed. Nevertheless, racism persisted for some time in certain private sectors, aimed towards the "Chinks" or "heathen Chinee."

It was a free Friday afternoon when Allan and three other privates, all Chinese except for one Private MacMillan, decided to go into town for hamburgers still clad in their army olive drabs. New Venice restaurant had been highly recommended by Sergeant Pickering. It was easy to find. The group followed the welcoming aroma that wafted out into the street. Unfortunately, they were greeted at the entrance by a less-than-welcoming proprietor.

"We don't serve your kind here. The German guy can come in. You three have to leave."

MacMillan responded, "I'm not German! And, if my buddies can't eat here, neither will I." He turned to the three, "Let's go. We need to tell the Sarge this is a lousy place."

The foursome, without speaking at all, marched back to the base directly to Pickering's office. Sometimes silence communicates more than discourse when humans are linked by commonality of experience. A nod, a glance, and we know. (MacMillan actually knew Allan from growing up in the same neighborhood in Oakland, and so developed an affinity for Chinese friends. In fact, the two had made the decision together to enlist.)

Pickering was incensed. "Gentlemen, we're all going back there! Now! Shame on Joe. I eat there all the time, and I had no idea he would do such a thing." The now fivesome marched back to the restaurant.

The proprietor was particularly venomous in that he implied he'd rather serve a German than a Chinese. There was such antipathy towards America's chief enemy on the Western Front of the war that many American restaurants even disdained the German word "hamburger" and changed it to "liberty sandwich" on their menus. New Venice was no exception.

The owner, Joe, was out front again. "Sarge, how are y'all doing this lovely day?"

"Not so good, Joe. Not so good. Listen. I understand you turned away my men here."

Joe crossed his arms. "Well, not all of 'em."

"Joe, y'know what I meant. These here are American GIs no matter where they came from. You see their uniforms? They serve to protect us. They serve to protect this here establishment of yours, too. Now listen, Joe. Do me a favor and give these four gentlemen a table. And, if I hear any trouble, I'll order the whole base to stop eating here. And I can do that." Pickering gave his soldiers a mechanical salute, turned, and marched off.

Joe did not say a word, but reluctantly waved the four into the restaurant and pointed at a table in the back corner. "Son, take care 'o these boys!"

The young man, perhaps in his late teens, came to the table and was much more hospitable than his father and even very polite, addressing each of them as "Sir."

As the foursome finished up and paid the bill, Allan left an extra five-dollar bill on the table. His buddies protested, but Allan explained, "I waited tables before. It's hard work and the boy was nice to us. Besides, watch what happens the next time we come back."

A few weeks later, Allan and his friends appeared at New Venice again. The same young man that waited on them before rushed out of the kitchen, "Dad, can I serve them? Can I? Can I? Please?"

***

It was simply a matter of enough idle time on the weekends that Allan and a number of his buddies eventually discovered each other's musical faculties.

In addition to the violin, Allan had also learned to play the *zhongruan* (a four-stringed plucked instrument more often called a "Chinese mandolin") in school. But in his futile search for such a foreign instrument in Florida, he found and settled for a second-hand banjo, which he successfully tamed into behaving and almost sounding like a Chinese mandolin.

The weekend jam sessions, comprised of anywhere from four to as many as ten performers and their respective instruments, created a unique fusion of Chinese and American music. By osmosis, Allan also learned to play the piano and guitar from his new accompanists in these sessions. Eventually, they evolved into a full ensemble that played regularly every weekend, providing much appreciated entertainment for the barracks. They were even invited to perform at the officers' quarters several times. Most of the time, Allan was the soloist on the instrument that he loved and played best, the violin.

MAY LIN

On October 20, 1944, Allan returned to the Presidio of Monterey, California, to receive his honorable discharge. At 5'4" and 120 pounds, he had not been able to pass the physical demands for air or combat duty. But, he performed his assignments in ground support with utmost diligence and commitment.

In addition to his discharge certificate, he was rewarded with something far more precious. There in Monterey, crowded in a small room along with about a dozen other Chinese soldiers, he held up his right hand. *"I hereby declare, on oath, that I absolutely and entirely renounce and abjure all allegiance and fidelity to any foreign prince, potentate, state, or sovereignty, and particularly to China, of which I have heretofore been a subject or citizen; that I will support and defend the Constitution and laws of the United States of America against all enemies, foreign and domestic; that I will bear true faith and allegiance to the same; and that I take this obligation freely, without any mental reservation or purpose of evasion; so help me God."*

Having served the requisite two years, Allan was now recognized as a United States citizen.

After two years away, he was happy to return to live with his Uncle Som, his aunt, and cousins in Oakland. They were just as ecstatic for his return. The first evening back, he and his cousins chatted far into the night, just like the first night when he arrived from China five years earlier. There was so much to catch up on. Lily was particularly pleased that the entire evening's conversations were in English. "Allan, your English has become as good as ours. Remember our first night when you arrived?"

He smiled at himself, quite proud of his advancement. "Yes, but I still feel like I have so much to learn. I get very confused sometimes. Why does a man call his girlfriend 'Baby' when she's a grown-up? And in Chinese, we say 'close the light,' but here I have to say 'turn off the light?' I figured out when I really like something, I'm supposed to call it 'the cat's meow.'" The entire evening was punctuated with hearty laughter.

But when everyone retired to bed, he again became acutely aware of the void in his life. He still clung to that last letter from Sin Wong, which had seen many Army uniform pockets in the last two years. Throughout those two years he persisted in sending letters out from the air base, but the war was not over and the Japanese muzzling of communications continued. So he never received any replies.

Allan was able to return to his old job at House of Lee. In fact, he returned to a surprise welcome back party that even included many of his favorite customers. He was showered profusely with congratulations and gratitude for his service to the country.

That evening, after closing up, the employees sat down to their usual dinner cobbled together from the leftover ingredients before going home. Allan was very glad to finally have Chinese food again . . . Chinese American food, at least.

The very same Philco radio that three years earlier blared the fright and panic of war into the restaurant was now exuding Glenn Miller's soothing "Moonlight Serenade."

May Lin, one of the chef's daughters who had been working there for some time took a seat next to Allan. "Allan, will you stay behind for a while? I have something to ask you."

"Can you ask me now?"

"Let's talk after everyone leaves."

May Lin was very quiet through the meal. After everyone left, Allan started, "What's on your mind?"

"You know, I missed you very badly when you went into the Army. I was so worried for you, and I'm so glad you returned safely."

"I'm glad, too. But I did ground support at the air base, so I was never in any danger."

"I remember you used to always talk about your wife in China. Have you heard from her?"

"Not since her last letter. That was about five years ago."

"Do you know if she's even alive anymore? The Japanese killed many women, too."

"I don't know. I hope she's alive."

"Allan, I think you've always known I care very much for you. I don't want to see you waste your life waiting for someone who may never come back."

Allan stood up, "No, May Lin, you cannot say that. You don't know, and I don't know. But as long as I haven't heard anything to the contrary, I am still a married man. And I still have a daughter and a mother."

May Lin blinked and her eyes effused a cascade of tears. "While you were gone, I went out with a number of men, but none of them were as kind and caring as you are. I think you should be realistic."

"May Lin, this is very awkward for me to say. You are a beautiful girl, and you're also very kind and sweet. I'd be lying if I said I wasn't attracted to you. But I still have to wait until the war is over to learn of the fate of my family back in Canton. I'm sorry, May Lin. I have to get home. You need to get home and rest, too."

"Promise me, Allan." She wiped her watery eyes with her bare fingers. "Promise me. I'll wait. Let me know when you get any news."

"I need to get home, May Lin. Sleep well. And, thank you for putting the party together. I did really appreciate it."

"So, you knew."

"Of course."

***

Japan was unrelenting. Although the European theater had by April of 1945 wound down with the surrender of Nazi Germany and the Axis, Japan persisted. Still continuing to suffer many casualties, both military and civilian, throughout the Pacific islands, Emperor Hirohito refused to yield to pressures to surrender, even pressure from his own advisors and virtually the entire war-weary Japanese citizenry. By the end of summer, President Truman evaluated a land invasion of Japan (code named Operation Downfall, it still was not given high expectation of a quick end to the war). Anticipating massive Japanese civilian casualties (five to ten million people) along with probably huge American and Allied military casualties (estimated as high as four million soldiers), Truman and his numerous advisors instead made the difficult decision to drop the world's first atomic bomb on what was at the time a major military installation and munitions stockyard, Hiroshima. The bomb was dropped on August 6, 1945, and the devastation was like no other man-made event the world had ever seen before.

But, this still did not in the least bit discourage the stubborn Hirohito, even with many of his military advisors begging for surrender. It was not until three days later, August 9, when the second atomic bomb was dropped, this time on Nagasaki, followed by the threat of a conventional carpet bombing raid on Tokyo, before Hirohito finally relented and announced that Japan would accept the Allies' demands. (In the end, the casualties were estimated to be about one hundred thousand Japanese along with a handful of captured American and Allied soldiers on the ground.) Three weeks later, on September 2, 1945, Japan officially surrendered aboard the USS *Missouri*.

World War II was finally over on both the Western and Pacific fronts.

THE TELEGRAM

At the end of the war, it had been more than six years since Allan last heard from his wife. Was May Lin right? Had Sin Wong, their daughter, and his mother all perished by the hands of Japanese soldiers? Was he being foolish "waiting for Godot?" Some of his friends, not just May Lin, had also urged him to abandon his hopes and start a new life and a new family here in America. But he held fast, clinging to the letter that had become the conduit to the happiness he felt the day he married her. Every night, he would still caress that letter against his chest. The letter was now the personification of Sin Wong's real being.

In December of 1945, Congress rekindled Allan's last and fading glimmer of hope. It passed the War Brides Act. Signed into law on December 28, the act permitted all U.S. citizens, which now included Allan, to bring their wives to America as long as they were coming from an Allied country. But was this a vacuous victory for Allan?

No, he told himself.

Meantime, May Lin's continued affection for Allan had gotten more persistent. And Allan realized that the mutual attraction for each other was very real. They were exchanging awkward glances whenever they passed each other at work, and Allan was glad when their work shifts did not intersect.

Two magnets in close enough proximity inevitably and uncontrollably in a split-second slap together; it is an inviolable law of nature and the only remedy would be physical distance. Allan, frightened that his baser instincts could take over and in an instant of indiscretion overpower his pledge to his wife, felt he had to leave his job at House of Lee.

He was quickly hired by Teddy, who owned Teddy's Market, a small, corner grocery store, only half a block from his home on 8th Street. Teddy got to know and like Allan as a regular customer there over the years, and he admitted to Allan that, impressed by his honesty, he had always wanted to hire him as a clerk. Teddy distinctly remembered the time that he had accidentally given Allan too much change on a purchase, and Allan immediately pointed it out and returned the excess money.

Teddy also saw his initiative and industriousness once he started working at the market. When the shelves were fully stocked and no customers were present, Allan would dust the merchandise, wash the windows, sweep the sidewalk outside, or do whatever he could think of other than stand idle.

Tuesday started as a quiet, ordinary morning, December 17, 1946. Allan was behind the counter tidying the display of Bit-O-Honey and Payday candy bars while having one of his usual friendly small talks with a regular customer. Teddy was in the back room, perhaps doing bookkeeping or checking inventory.

Uncle Som suddenly burst through the entrance. The look on his face was different, not as though he was there merely to pick up a bottle of Carnation Milk or a loaf of Wonder Bread. "Your wife, Allan! Your wife! She just telegrammed!" He waved the evidence in circles in the air, a half sheet of yellow paper. Without courtesy, he rushed up to the counter, pushed the customer aside, and slapped the telegram hard onto the counter.

> . . . WE ARE ALL HEALTHY. POST SERVICE NOW OPEN. REPLY BACK BY WESTERN UNION IMMEDIATELY. SIN WONG.

Allan was stunned. His eyes, transfixed on the last two words of the telegram, "SIN WONG," instantly started watering. A teardrop seeped out from the corner of his left eye. Then his right eye. Then more tears. Then the dam broke. The torrent of tears came to a crescendo of sobs. It seemed a long time before his mind could fully grasp the reality of the news. His voice quivered, "Thank you, Uncle, thank you, thank you!" By then, Uncle Som had already dashed into the backroom to report the news to Teddy.

Teddy came charging out. "Allan, I'm so happy for you. You take the day off. Go home and celebrate. Besides, it's Christmastime. What a gift that you are so deserving of!"

Uncle Som offered, "I need to take you to the Western Union office right now."

Teddy was physically pushing Allan out the door. "Go! Go now before they close!" It was still morning, but everyone was in a confused celebratory frenzy.

THE REUNION

It was as if time had come to a stop the moment Allan stepped off the gangplank in Canton. The planets had stopped orbiting. The Earth had ceased spinning on its axis. When Allan and Sin Wong's eyes locked in instant recognition, they darted into each other's arms and engaged in an inseparable grip. That and a deluge of tears made spoken words inadequate and even unnecessary. But, as quickly as they had embraced, Allan's mother physically separated the young couple, scolding them that they were in public. Such overt acts outdoors were considered immodest in that time and culture. Sin Wong was immediately embarrassed and looked down at the ground, whereas Allan, after seven years in America, had grown accustomed to such overt public affection. His cousins, Lily and Flora, had taken him to see *Casablanca* twice.

He knelt down to eye level with the little seven-year-old girl and spoke to her in Cantonese, "You've been obedient to your mother?"

She replied in Cantonese in a faint and timid little voice, "Yes."

"Say 'yes, Ah Baba' and louder," Sin Wong corrected.

So Jing complied, "Ngaw ho teng gow, Ah Baba." [I've been very obedient, Daddy.] Allan was as elated to hear those words as he was to see his bride and mother. He drew a deep breath, choking back so as to not allow tears in front of his little daughter.

Because the United States government did not recognize Chinese civil marriages, on February 21, 1947, Allan took his bride to the American Consulate in Canton to marry her again, this time under American law. Of course, he was more than proud to do so, now as an American citizen. The entire ceremony was officiated in five minutes with only Allan, Sin Wong, and two government officials in the small office. It was a spartan office filled with uncheerful green metal furniture and squeaky uncomfortable chairs, and the only departure from the drab was the brilliant red, white, and blue American flag pinned to the wall. In an instant, Allan recognized the look, feel, and smell of this very austere chamber reminiscent of the exact environment where he had had his interrogation eight years earlier on Angel Island. He contently grinned, reminding himself that that was then and this is now.

Although missing the raucous pomp and fanfare of their first wedding in his farm village, the two were garbed for this occasion. Sin Wong once again donned the butterfly embroidered red silk cheongsam she had worn for their first ceremony. Allan made it a point to bring back with him his father's silk vest that his mother had presented to him the night before he left for Gum Shan and wore it along with a suit and tie which were a bon voyage gift from his proud cousins Lily, Flora, and Quong.

That evening, there was a small family celebratory dinner at the Gee household. In addition to Allan and his wife, daughter, and mother, there were Sin Wong's mother and stepbrother, See Chew. It was then that Allan learned that Sin Wong's father was a direct casualty of the war itself. While Allan knew that his father-in-law had died while he was gone, he had not known the exact circumstances . . . he had taken his own life.

Sin Wong's father had built the thriving cane furniture factory from the ground up. She knew it meant everything to him. It was his life, his purpose. It validated him as a good provider. But, neither she nor her mother could understand why he had to take his own life. Perhaps it was simply too much horror and grief for him when he watched, hiding behind a large rock, the dozen or so Japanese soldiers come with flame throwers to surround the large building and torch his creation, building and content, to nothing but ashes on level ground. He felt the fierce heat of the destructive and voracious conflagration. He heard the intermittent hostile roaring of the flame throwers switching on and off. He was utterly confused by the aggressors' cacophonic shouts in a completely foreign language. The large wooden building crackled and creaked and finally toppled. The once invigorating aroma of freshly woven wet cane was instantly vaporized into acrid eye-burning and lung-searing fumes.

Perhaps it was simply too horrifying to witness all this. Or perhaps he reasoned that, unable to any longer be a provider, he should no longer be a consumer. Not only had he been a provider for his own family; he had provided livelihoods for the many he had employed. Perhaps the reasons were much deeper.

Over what should have been a joyful celebration, Sin Wong tearfully recounted that tragic day. Until that fateful day, she had never seen her father cry before. She recounted being horrifically frightened to see him stumble home, red eyes filled with tears, and exploding, "The Japanese! The Japanese! It's all gone! My factory! They destroyed it all!" And the next morning, the family found him drained white and lifeless, cold and inert, still clutching an empty brown ceramic vial. Rationally, Sin Wong knew he had taken the poison. But through the rest of her life, she considered it murder on the part of the Japanese.

At the end of the dinner, Allan was also a bearer of bad news. He had to explain that the War Brides Act allowed him to only take his wife back to America . . . but no one else.

There was anticipation that the communists would soon blanket even southern China. Fortunately, Allan had brought enough money to move his mother, his mother-in-law, So Jing, and his brother-in-law along with his family to Hong Kong, still then a British colony. But he could not promise how long they would have to wait before he could bring them to America. He did promise that he would one day bring them all to Gum Shan, but he didn't promise when.

This time he knew better than to make a time commitment.

THE USS *GENERAL W.H. GORDON*

The Chinese name for the Pacific Ocean, *Tai Ping Yong,* is a direct translation from "Pacific," meaning peaceful and calm. The tranquil June seas indeed lived up to the ocean's namesake in stark contrast to Allan's first trek crossing the Pacific eight years earlier. The calm seas made the journey physically much more agreeable this time. Not only that, but now as a returning American citizen, Allan no longer had the dreadful anxiety and apprehensions he held as an aspiring paper son. He did not even mind still being in steerage as long as he had his bride with him.

In the daytime, they would stroll the deck of the USS *General W.H. Gordon,* pausing occasionally at the railings. Sometimes they would stop at the bow where Allan would explain to Sin Wong what to expect and look forward to in Gum Shan. Sometimes they would lean over the stern to contemplate the rapidly growing separation from their motherland. Other times, they would just linger over the port or starboard side railing, watching the ephemeral free form doilies of foam lazily appearing and then disappearing into the satiny waters lapping at the hull. The rhythmic gurgling and sloshing of water as the ship bobbed through the waves was soothing to the both of them. Occasionally, in the first few days, an albatross would traverse the gray cumulus clouds overhead.

These moments were calming to Sin Wong. She had been particularly despondent having to leave behind their daughter, her mother, and mother-in-law.

A week into their crossing, their reverie was compounded by the exciting news that they would be bringing into their world their first American-born child. Sin Wong was pregnant.

Their exultation was short-lived. Allan and Sin Wong, along with the ship's medic, initially dismissed her bouts of severe discomfort as seasickness combined with morning sickness. But several more days into the trip Sin Wong had a dreadful foreboding about her three-month pregnancy.

And their hope was indeed dashed. The baby was not to be.

In spite of the initial anticipation of the bright promises Gum Shan would offer, Sin Wong was now difficult to comfort. She was still in anguish over her father's suicide. Her nightmares of Japanese soldiers outside her home and their fighter planes zooming within feet overhead returned and menaced her sleep every night. And she began missing the only people she knew as family, save for a husband she was just getting to know. She only found comfort in realizing that he was willing to violate the ship's rules and sneak into the infirmary to spend every night by her side.

She would abruptly sit up in her sleep shouting, "The Japanese! We must hide! They're coming!"

Allan would immediately embrace her and whisper, "Wake up, Sin. It's only a bad dream. You're safe now, Sin. We're on a ship on our way to Gum Shan."

And, it was then that she was assured that he was a compassionate man.

In the bed next to hers was another woman, Gim Ngook Fong, who was brought to the infirmary because of severe seasickness. Allan and Sin Wong learned that she was traveling alone on her way to San Francisco to reunite with her husband, whom she had not seen in eleven years. One night, she complained of being very cold. Allan took off his coat and made a second blanket with it for her. She rolled over and told Sin Wong, "You are a very lucky wife. I've been watching. He's very kind." Then she turned to Allan, "I'll return your coat in the morning."

"No, you keep it to stay warm until we get to San Francisco."

Through the remainder of the voyage, the three became very acquainted with each other. Allan scurried about in the daytime bringing both women tea and other necessities. In the night, he would continue with his attentiveness, although surreptitiously.

Sin Wong's confinement to the infirmary turned out to be a blessing in disguise. Although the Chinese Exclusion Act had been by statute repealed, the momentum of governmental attitudes fostered by the now defunct law persisted. Throughout the USS *General W.H. Gordon,* immigration officials continued to interrogate her Chinese passengers looking for possible instances of fraud. Either out of administrative oversight or maybe even compassion, the onboard INS officials neglected to investigate any passengers in the infirmary. Allan himself was subjected to questioning, but he merely had to produce his passport, military discharge papers, and immunization records to satisfy the INS official. (By late 1947, the Chinese Americans in San Francisco challenged Congress, querying why Chinese war brides were still subjected to onboard interrogation while the European war brides were admitted freely. As a result, INS was later given a cease and desist order from the State Department on these interrogations.)

Soon, seagulls were in sight swooping and gliding gracefully against the calm azure blue skies, squawking at each other in their own language only they could understand among themselves. Sin Wong beamed a smile broader than Allan had seen in weeks when he returned below decks to report that the bird sightings signified they were close to Gum Shan.

As the steamer approached the San Francisco Bay, Allan helped his bride up to the main deck, so that she could look up and see the welcoming belly of the Golden Gate Bridge as they ceremoniously sailed under. He wanted her to feel the same exhilaration he experienced eight years ago. The two embraced and Allan's shoulder became tear-soaked.

Upon disembarking in San Francisco, there was mob confusion whereby Gim Ngook was swallowed into the anonymity of an anthill of passengers and receiving families. She was not to be seen by Allan and Sin Wong again. At least, not for many years. And Allan was not concerned about losing a coat.

SAV MOR LIQUOR STORE

Allan was surprised to see Teddy show up at Teddy's Market just as he was starting his morning shift. This worried him. Had something gone wrong? Did the cash register not balance from the night before when he closed? Was he being fired?

"Allan, I am thinking of retiring very soon. And, I can't think of anyone harder working and more deserving of buying me out. You would do this business proud. So, I want you to have first say before I put the store up for sale."

Instantly Allan remembered Mr. Lee's prophetic words, "One day, I want to see you own a business, too," when he first went to work at House of Lee.

"Teddy, I'm honored that you would consider me. I would want this opportunity more than anything else. But, I don't have the means to buy you out. I just finished paying off my paper to my sponsor. And now I have to send money to Hong Kong every month to support my daughter and other family members."

"I don't need you to pay me all at once. I'll take a down payment. Then you can pay me monthly from your profits."

"Thank you. But I don't think my savings is even enough for a down payment right now." Allan paused for a long moment. "Let me go home and see what I can put together. Can we talk about this again tomorrow?" Allan's mind was racing now. He so badly hungered for this opportunity. He was thrilled at the thought of being a business owner. And he was confident he could do it well. He had watched Teddy over the years keep the books, negotiate discounts from the wholesalers, balance the till, make payroll, and pay the bills. He did many shifts entirely on his own. And during those shifts particularly, he indeed fantasized being the boss. If only he had the wherewithal to buy Teddy over.

"Of course, Allan. Take a few days. This is a big commitment, but I know you could do the job. The regulars [customers] know and like you here." That, of course, made Allan want it even more. It was a source of gratification when he could make customers happy. He realized this from the time he waited tables at House of Lee.

"How much do you want for a down payment? And how much must I pay you each month?"

"I was planning on listing it for $13,000. But, I'll take $12,500 if you're the one buying it. Why don't you see what you can come up with and let me know? My wife and I don't need a lot of monthly income." "But I would like to be paid off in five years at most." Teddy had over the years acquired a number of apartment buildings throughout the Bay Area that would support their retirement comfortably.

Allan cradled his cup of coffee for a long while spinning it back and forth on its saucer without taking a sip. His pensive stare at the Chase & Sanborn coffee tin on the stove was finally interrupted by Sin Wong's voice, "Your coffee is getting cold, but you look like you must have a lot on your mind. What are you thinking about?"

He laid out the entire opportunity to her. "Well, what do you think?" It was rare in those times for a man to ask for his wife's opinion on business matters, but he realized the decision would affect the both of them.

He finally took a sip of his coffee. "My coffee is cold!"

"Here, let me get you another cup."

"But, Sin, what do you think?"

"What do you mean, what do I think? Of course, you have to take it! Isn't this why we left China? We will find a way to pay for it. You go tell Teddy today before he decides to sell to someone else or decides he wants the full $13,000 from you! You don't want to be an employee all your life, do you?"

"No, of course I don't." But Allan realized the arithmetic did not add up. With what little they could gather for a down payment, the monthly payments over five years would be more than the profit the store could produce.

Sin Wong was daring and commanding. "You go and tell Teddy today that you will buy the store. I'll figure something out."

***

Sin Wong had secretly gone to Uncle Som to plead their case. Not only had Allan paid back Uncle Som for his paper in full; he paid it back ahead of schedule by paying more whenever he had extra cash. She reminded Uncle Som of this, and he was not at all reluctant to loan Allan the down payment. "Your husband has proven he's good for his word. And, of course, as with us Chinese always, I don't want interest. He can pay me back whenever he can. He's a good boy and I just want to see him successful." The down payment he gave was generous beyond expectation.

Even then, the monthly payments to Teddy would still be onerous. Allan understood the seasonal fluctuation of this business. What if there were months when profits were much less than the payment?

Allan and Sin Wong had become good friends with Mr. and Mrs. Gin, who owned Gin's Liquor on the corner of Franklin and 9th Streets in Oakland Chinatown. Mr. Gin advised Allan that liquor provided a much higher profit margin than groceries. Hence, Allan appealed to the California ABC (Alcoholic Beverage Control) Board and was successful at purchasing a liquor license with $3,000 cash, since Uncle Som had loaned them much more than was needed for the actual down payment. Now he was in the grocery and liquor business.

Thus, the large red block letters that spelled Teddy's Market on the wall on the parking lot side of the building at 93 8th Street were painted over to boldly announce Sav Mor Liquor Store. On June 1, 1948, a mere one year since returning from China, the twenty-nine-year-old Allan posed proudly behind the counter of his very own business for a grand opening photo.

And Sin Wong was six months pregnant.

FIRST GENERATION AMERICAN

On September 13, Allan and Sin Wong became the proud parents of their first American-born child, Jennie Gee, at Providence (aptly named) Hospital in Oakland. They gave her the Chinese name "So Ping" perhaps in reference to the Pacific Ocean *(Tai Ping Yong)* as a remembrance of the unborn child lost while crossing the Pacific.

Within six months of the grand opening, Sav Mor Liquor Store proved so successful and Jennie had brought them so much joy that they decided to add to the family. On August 26, 1949, Carolyn, So Yin, was born, also at Providence Hospital. Both babies were delivered by Dr. Jacob Yee, the only bilingual Chinese doctor practicing western medicine in Oakland Chinatown at the time.

After each delivery, Sin Wong complained to Allan, "It was good that Dr. Yee could speak Chinese with me through the deliveries, but when he turned to the nurses to speak in English, I felt very left out."

"Sin, we are now in America. I want you to start attending school to learn English. Everything will start to be easier for you if you speak English. You can take the bus anywhere you want, you can shop anywhere outside of Chinatown, and you won't feel left out of these conversations."

"How do I learn? Would you teach me?"

"I'll take you to the same school I went to here in Chinatown."

Allan would take her to the Oakland Chinese Community Center in Chinatown where they taught English to immigrants every Tuesday and Thursday nights. Other nights, they would watch television together, so that they could both improve their language skills. He would have to explain to her why he was laughing so heartily at Milton Berle or Morey Amsterdam. Together, they would enjoy the weekly featured talents on *The Ed Sullivan Show*.

"After you improve your English enough, Sin, I want you to study for your American citizenship. When you become a U.S. citizen, everything will be much better for you. We can get you life insurance, you can vote, and soon you can drive. It will also be easier if you ever want to get a job after we're done raising our children."

"Speaking of children, there is one thing that I'm worried about."

"What else would worry you, Sin?"

"I don't want our children to lose our history and culture. I want them to always know and respect the Chinese way."

"Of course, we are not giving anything up, Sin. We are only adding things. In addition to speaking English, there are many good qualities about American life that we can embrace without losing our Chinese way—we will always honor the elderly, we will always put a high value on education, and we will always respect hard work, patience, and modesty.

"And, I do want them to speak Chinese at home, Sin. I'm not worried about their learning English; that will happen when they go to school. I learned most of my English in the Army."

"Your cousins, Lily and Flora, have said the same things to me, Suey Fong. I do want to learn English myself, and I do want to become an American citizen."

Strolling the south bank of the Pearl River in
China with schoolmate, Soon Goh. c1934.

Allan (second from left) with his sponsoring family in
Oakland, California. c1940.

Youthful portrait. Oakland,
California. c1940.

Youthful portrait. Oakland,
California. c1940.

Featured violin soloist. (Unknown newspaper.)

Venice Army Airfield in Venice, Florida.
Allan is center. c1943.

Certificate of Witness to Marriage

(See Section 72, title 22 of the United States Code)

FOREIGN SERVICE OF THE UNITED STATES

American Consulate General,

Canton, China; March 6, 1947

I, Harold G. McConeghey, Vice Consul of the United States of America at Canton, China, do hereby certify that on this twenty-first day of February, A. D. 19 47, at 27 Fook Hing Road, Shameen, in the city of Canton, China,

Gee Suay Fong, a CITIZEN of the United States, aged 29 years, born in Lee Hing Lee, Toishan, Kwangtung, China and now residing in 115 8th St., Oakland, California, and

Wong Sun, a CITIZEN of the Republic of China, aged 25 years, born in Foo Sun Chuen, Toishan, Kwangtung, China, and now residing in Foo Sun Chuen, Toishan, Kwangtung, China, were united in marriage in my presence.

In witness whereof, I have hereunto subscribed my name and affixed the seal of my office at Canton, China, this sixth day of March, A. D. 19 47, and of the Independence of the United States the one hundred and seventieth.

Harold G. McConeghey

Vice Consul of the United States of America.

Fee: One in Quadruplicate.

Service No. 726

MAR 19 1947

Certificate of Marriage under American law, issued at the
American Consulate in Canton, China. 1947.

LIST OR MANIFEST OF ALIEN PASSENGERS FOR THE UNITED

Coming home to America. Page from USS General W.H. Gordon passenger manifest showing Allan (Suey Fong) and Sin Wong as passengers #17 and #18, respectively. 1947.

Left to right: Jennie, Lester (the author), Allan, and his 1947 Buick Roadmaster. Oakland, California. 1951.

Proud owner of Sav Mor Liquor Store #1. Oakland, California.

Front porch of first home they owned.
Left to right: Edna, Allan, Lester (the author), Sin Wong,
Jennie, and Carolyn. Oakland, California. c1953.

Sin Wong's Certificate of American citizenship. 1956.

Portrait in Athol Avenue house.
Oakland, California. c1958.

Entire family on vacation. Left to right: Allan,
Sin Wong, Lester (the author), Emma (below),
Sylvia, Jennie, Edna, and Carolyn. c1959.

Sin Wong and Allan vacationing in scenic Guilin, China. c1995.

Recognition for community service through the Gee Family Association by San Francisco Mayor Willie Brown. San Francisco, California. 2002.

*Second term as president of the Gee Family
Association. San Francisco, California. c2004.*

*With second wife, Elaine, at Lester's home.
San Francisco, California. c2009.*

Part Two

"That which I do for myself will one day die with me. But that which I do for others will live on forever."

—AUTHOR UNKNOWN

MY FIRST FIVE YEARS

It was a Friday. April 13, 1951. It was around noon Pacific Time, so there was never any doubt that anywhere in United States it was a Friday the Thirteenth.

I, Lester Allan Gee, came into this world.

Years later, I was often told by Dr. Jacob Yee, the family doctor, that I was the "lucky child" because I was the first one to ride home from the hospital in the first automobile my father ever purchased. Dad often spoke proudly of his 1947 Buick Roadmaster. He bought it used, but it was his.

I was also told that, when I was born, the five of us were cozily "sardined" into the one, same bedroom that Dad inhabited when he first moved in with his sponsoring family on 8th Street. And, of course, we shared the entire house with "Grandpa" Som and his family. My bassinet was fashioned out of one of the drawers pulled out from a chest.

I have no actual personal recollection of having lived there, although I do remember later visiting often to see my Grandpa

Som; his wife, Say Paw; and Uncle Quong, Auntie Lily, and Auntie Flora.

By the time I could remember much of my early childhood, Dad had bought our first house at 1101 5ᵗʰ Avenue. Dad was always keenly proud that his military service granted him his American citizenship. But now he was even more proud and grateful as he bragged that, being a veteran, he was able to purchase this first home through the Veteran's Administration. It was a duplex, enabling him to collect rent from the family living in the upstairs unit.

The husband living upstairs was an Oakland Police officer, making it convenient for Mom to discipline us. "If you don't behave, the *luhk yee* upstairs will come and get you!" We children fell in line very quickly. And, whenever the three of us were sent upstairs to be babysat, we must have been as disciplined as Terra Cotta Warriors.

Now, being several miles away from his store, Dad was no longer able to simply walk the half a block to and from work. Thus, citing the need for a more reliable automobile, he rationalized purchasing his first brand new car, a 1952 Buick Super, for $2,000 cash. That was a large sum then, but the business was doing well, and Mom and Dad lived very frugally otherwise. New cars eventually became the one and only material frivolity he ever allowed himself. Was it the exhilarating smell of newness? Did he simply welcome each fascinating new feature year by year? An automatic transmission, air conditioning, power windows? Perhaps it was all of these trivial indulgences. But was there something much more profound? It was perhaps in his mind a symbolic manifestation of the promise of Gum Shan—he had propelled himself to escape velocity and left far behind the gravity of rickety rickshaws and smelly ox-drawn carts on the rugged dirt roads of Kee Hing Lee.

Mom and Dad furnished this first home with mostly secondhand, maybe even thirdhand, furniture. The red Naugahyde that covered the seat of a squeaky rocker had a clean split in the middle that occasionally oozed yellowed cotton stuffing and puffed little dust clouds whenever we bounced on it. We did have the luxury of a television set that Dad bought from a friend who was in trouble, although Mom scolded him for such an extravagance. It was a large scratched-up wooden cabinet with a tiny screen in the center directly above the letters RCA. The back panel was missing, enabling me to peer behind the set to see where Mighty Mouse had flown off to (all I saw back there was the orange glow of vacuum tubes, which I sometimes thought were more visually exciting than the black-and-white images of Jack Benny.)

I remember the randomly abrupt bursts of whirring from the electric Singer sewing machine that Mom sat at to produce much of our clothing. She would often disrupt our play to have us try on various partially completed articles of clothing, while commenting, "Why would we spend extra money on ready-made clothing when the material is so much cheaper?"

After each meal, the leftovers were always neatly covered with wax paper. Mom would declare, "We cannot waste food. There are children in China who are starving. All they have is plain white rice just to fill their stomachs." And the wax paper was reused until it ripped.

Dad's spartan childhood and Mom's newly impoverished life as a result of the war had taught them a frugality that would follow them even through their most abundant years. (One of our sons as a teenager came back from a visit and reported to us, "Grandma took a spoon and just scraped off and threw out the top layer of moldy jam and told us the rest of the strawberry jam was too good to waste. We would have just tossed out the whole jar, wouldn't we?")

In due time, I realized I had new younger sister. Edna was born in January 1952, again at Providence Hospital as all of us were.

Our youngest sister, Emma, was born in November 1956. Mom proclaimed, "This has been a truly special year. This is the year I became an American citizen, and now I have my last baby."

Over the previous years, since arriving in America, Mom had continued going to night school as far back as I could recall. I also remember Mr. Lau, the rotund chain-smoking tutor who regularly came to our home with an enormous briefcase to prepare Mom for the U.S. Constitution exam, a requirement for becoming an American citizen (in addition to competency in the English language.) Along with the books he extracted from his briefcase for Mom, he always pulled out a pad of paper and a pencil to keep me occupied making drawings at the table during Mom's lessons. I somehow remembered many of the facts Mom was reciting to Mr. Lau; I was learning by osmosis. There are three branches of government: the legislative, the judicial, and the executive branches. Each state elects two senators to Congress. There are nine judges that make up the Supreme Court.

July 20, 1956, was a momentous day for Mom, as I later realized. I remember Mom and Dad coming home and excitedly showing us a piece of paper. At the time, it may have meant more to my older sisters, as I was too young to appreciate that she had just been sworn in as a naturalized U.S. citizen that day, and she was proudly waving her Certificate of Naturalization. I may have been more excited that Mr. Lau would no longer be coming by to pollute our home, leaving behind an ashtray full of wet cigarette butts and foul-smelling air.

But 1956 was also a special year for me. That fall, I started kindergarten at Lincoln Elementary School, located just a few blocks away from Sav Mor Liquor. I have a vivid memory of my first day. Mom was home, tending to Edna and newborn Emma, while Dad drove us to school on his way to work. Jennie and Carolyn jumped out of the car and were quickly swallowed into the cacophonic sea of many other children. But Dad took my hand and walked me to my classroom. He greeted my teacher, told me I would not see him until school was over, and then left. Sometime later in the morning, when Mrs. Ayres marched us out to the playground to teach us how to play Simon Says, I spotted through the Cyclone fence Dad's car still parked in the same spot when he dropped me off. Scanning the sidewalk, I spotted Dad leaning against the fence, fingers curled around the metal wires and squinting in the bright sunlight . . . watching me. He told Mom later that day he never went to work.

SAV MOR LIQUOR STORES NUMBER 2 AND 3

Soon after Emma was born, the two-bedroom home on 5th Avenue became clearly too small to accommodate two parents and five children. And being across the street from the Wonder Bread bakery, we were awakened every morning by delivery trucks that would noisily rumble in and out when it was still dark outside. Mom also complained that we were on a busy street with no safe place for us to play outdoors. (There was no backyard to this house.)

By then, Dad had acquired an additional store, which he aptly dubbed "Sav Mor Liquor Store Number 2," on Grove Street (which street has since been renamed Martin Luther King Way.) Thus, he had the additional income to trade up to our next home at 463 Athol Avenue. This was a four-bedroom, two-level Craftsman style house in a quiet upscale neighborhood on the hilly side of Lake Merritt. We children enjoyed much more room and, more important, a large and fenced-in backyard. It also particularly pleased Mom and Dad that the grammar school, Cleveland Elementary, was only a block away. (That was, of course, the very reason they had chosen this neighborhood.)

Soon after moving into the Athol house, Dad sold his original store on 8ᵗʰ Street and split the proceeds to buy two more stores. The new location on East Tennyson Road in Hayward was then designated as "Sav Mor Liquor Store Number 1," and his third store on Market Street in Oakland then became, of course, "Sav Mor Liquor Store Number 3."

Because of the many miles he would then travel from store to store, he acquired the habit of trading in for a new car every two or three years. And eventually, he advanced from standard sedans to luxury models, such as the Buick Electra and Cadillacs. Many of Mom's friends were judgmental, telling her that Dad was being too extravagant. I remember and admired Mom's defense of him. "He doesn't smoke, he doesn't drink, and he doesn't gamble. He can enjoy a new car anytime he wants."

I remember Auntie Jen, our nextdoor neighbor on Athol Avenue who often visited Mom for coffee. She also occasionally babysat us.

I liked her much because, being American, she helped Mom better understand many of the notions we children were bringing home from school that still bewildered her, such notions as Halloween and Christmas, which were unheard of in China. Auntie Jen also confirmed much of what Dad was trying to get Mom to understand about American culture.

I believe Mom was suspicious, as any wary parent should be, when we children told her we were supposed to receive presents at Christmastime. A lot of presents.

Auntie Jen had taught Mom how to set up a Christmas tree with lights. She had given us many decorations that she was no longer using, such as a large figure of Santa Claus and an electric menorah (which in later life I laughed about as Auntie Jen was not Jewish herself. Nor, obviously, were we.) Of course, the best part of Christmas would be all the nicely wrapped presents under the tree!

Later, I learned that Christmas was originally a Christian holiday. Yet, we were not a Christian family. Nevertheless, today I realize that all families need traditional rituals. However authentic or spurious as others may judge our practices, the traditional Christmas rituals that are repeatedly performed, albeit secular, give rise and significance to familial legacy.

We continue the ritual of gift-giving as we all realize it is the time of year to make each other's wishes come true. It is the time when family members who are too busy or too far away to finally break bread together and remember what the word "family" means. It becomes the time of charity. (I was struck by a memorable sign in a friend's home, "You don't need to be a Christian. You just need to be Christianly.")

We were, in retrospect, very thankful for Auntie Jen and the many other of Mom and Dad's American friends who made it easier for us to grow up bicultural.

Mom and Dad also assimilated politically. I would overhear them discussing various political issues, especially when it neared election time each year. They were naturally most concerned about issues that could affect their business. While it was important to Dad to vote on Election Day every November, Mom would usually go with him to vote only when it was a presidential election.

SUPPORTING TWO HOUSEHOLDS

Dad was glad to finally finish paying off Teddy and his Uncle Som. He would often acknowledge upon reflection, "Had it not been for them, we would not have all that we have today."

Mom would add kiddingly, "You'd still be gathering pig dung on the farm back in China."

But at some point, a certain conversation between Mom and Dad could no longer be ignored. Dad seldom complained about much, but he started. "It seems too often that your step-brother complains that I'm not sending them enough money. Now we're up to $200 a month going to Hong Kong! [In 1961, that was about $1,600 in today's dollars.] I've also been sending a little extra money for So Jing to continue with college. But we're not even sure if she is, in fact, in school."

Mom concurred immediately, "I've been thinking the same. Maybe now is the time to figure how to bring them all here. Not only are you supporting all of us here, you are supporting nine more people in Hong Kong." [Their daughter So Jing, Mom's mother, Dad's mother, and Mom's stepbrother's family of six.]

Mom continued, "If we bring them all here, you could put the adults to work. Maybe we've given them too much, and it's making it easy for them to be lazy and not work."

"I think you're right, Sin. I've spoiled them. But there are still a lot of obstacles. I might end up spending even more just on attorney's fees. And don't forget, even if we succeed with immigration, we still have to pay their airfare. Then, you know, we would probably have to support them at least temporarily once they get here.

I remember dreading each of the numerous times a Western Union courier would come to the door with an envelope. It always resulted in elevated voices from Mom and Dad. Not at each other, but at their frustration that every telegram was a request from Hong Kong for money because of one emergency or another. I read a few of them. "Mother very sick. Need $200." "Landlord needs us to move. Need $500."

It was Christmastime 1959. I remember a man perhaps in his early twenties who had been visiting us frequently. On this particular visit, I remember Dad saying to this man, "Stanley, we like you and trust you will take good care of our daughter. But we'd like to make one request."

"No problem. What is it?"

"We want you to quit smoking."

"I will do that."

The following year, Mom flew back to Hong Kong with Stanley along with a large sum of American Dollars zipped into one of her coat pockets. This cash paid for a wedding celebration for So Jing and Stanley. Dad had to stay behind to tend to his business and, of course, care for us. And this was one of those times Auntie Jen babysat us after school until Dad came home from work to cook for us.

It was then we children realized that Dad could cook too. And he was a very good cook. He explained to us that he had learned cooking while working at a restaurant when he first came to America.

"When I first arrived here, I was a busboy. Then when my English got better, I became a waiter. It was at the House of Lee on Fruitvale, and it's still there. I never worked in the kitchen, but I learned to cook just by watching."

Most of what he prepared was Chinese food, which I now realize was really Chinese American food. But, mornings he would cook American breakfasts, and some mornings he treated us to his incredible pancakes. They were so perfectly round that they would embarrass a compass . . . and they would rise to a full fluffy one inch. Even after Mom's return, we would beg him to make his pancakes many Saturday mornings. (And after I was married, Lila and I would enjoy "Dad's special hot-cakes" on many of our morning visits.)

Upon Mom's return to Oakland with the new bride and groom, we children all juggled our bedroom arrangements so that Stanley and Sylvia (So Jing's new American name designated by Stanley) had one of the bedrooms to themselves.

We didn't mind, as we were excited to finally meet our oldest sister. One of Mom's fondest stories of So Jing often repeated to us was from the war.

"We were running for the village gate with what belongings we could carry. We had been told that some women [bok gway paw—white ghost women] wearing red crosses would meet us at the gate and take us to a camp where we would be safe from the Japanese. I held your dad's mother's hand in one hand and tightly gripped your sister's hand in the other, leaving the house, when the Japanese planes suddenly and unexpectedly started buzzing overhead. Everyone ran screaming in all different directions in confusion, and the three of us gripped each other's hands even harder. On the way to the gate, we saw two children, a little boy and a little girl, both about the same age as your sister, holding each other's hands with no adult nearby, running, shouting, and crying, 'ah Mama! ah Baba!' over and over. So Jing shouted to me over the noise, 'Ah Mama, maybe they were misbehaving, so their mommy and daddy left them. You wouldn't leave me, would you? I'm very well behaved.' I gripped her hand even tighter and assured her, 'Precious one, I could never leave you.'" Mom would often finish the story with her eyes red and glistening.

Stanley was hired as a cashier at one of Dad's stores, and the couple lived with us until they had their first and only child, Nancy. It eventually became clearly too crowded for the ten of us in this four-bedroom house. Mom and Dad decided to purchase a fourplex in the Fruitvale area of Oakland, and asked Stanley and Sylvia, now with infant, to move into one of the apartment units and act as building manager in exchange for rent.

We children were glad to return to our previously more comfortable bedroom assignments. And Mom and Dad, as well as we children, immediately appreciated the reclaimed relative peace in our household again.

THE REST OF THE FAMILY

The Immigration and Nationality Act of 1965 (also known as the Hart-Celler Act) was signed into law by President Johnson after Congress passed it with 85 percent Republican support and 74 percent Democratic support. It essentially removed the last vestiges of the Chinese Exclusion Act so that Asian immigration was to be as liberal as European immigration. Even though the Chinese Exclusion Act was formally repealed in 1943, there was still a quota of no more than 105 Chinese immigrants per year. (Other nationalities at the same time had quotas as high as 60,000 per year.) But even after the Hart-Celler Act, priorities were assigned giving particular preference to reunification of immediate family members of American citizens and unfettered admission of professionals and those with specialized skills. Otherwise, "employability" became a criterion. Fortunately for many yet to come, Dad was in a strong position to guarantee employment for those who did not fall into any of the favored categories other than employability.

Now Mom and Dad had the legal capability to bring their respective mothers, as immediate family members, to America with fewer immigration issues. They would also be able to legally sponsor Mom's stepbrother, See Chew, and his entire family (he had his wife, Kim, and four children at the time) as long as he could be employed at any one of Dad's stores.

Dad had just purchased another liquor store in West Oakland, store Number 4. For the first time, the real estate was an optional part of the offer. While Dad primarily had his eyes on the business itself, Mom ultimately prevailed when they struggled with and argued for weeks over the purchase of the building, which in hindsight became an abundantly lucrative decision.

But, with the cost of this acquisition, Dad made clear that he certainly could not afford to bring everyone to America at the same time.

Nevertheless, it was time to juggle bedrooms again. In deference to Mom, Dad brought her mother, Yee Oi, to America first. Dad's mother would stay in Hong Kong to continue to help care for See Chew's children.

I remember Grandma Yee Oi initially as a welcomed addition to our household as she relieved Mom of many chores, both inside and outside the house. She helped with much of the cooking and cleaning, and even assisted Mom with the quite prolific vegetable garden in our large backyard.

But inevitably, interpersonal conflict reared its ugly head with Mom and Grandma. Mom had become too Americanized for her very doctrinaire, traditional (and short-tempered) mother to agree on many things.

Grandma never gave up scolding Mom for walking abreast of Dad. "You are not behaving like a proper wife. Walking alongside your husband, you might as well walk in front of him! You are so disrespectful!"

In China at that time, the wife must always walk behind the husband. But upon setting foot in America, Dad had instructed Mom, "You need not walk behind me. We are now in America. You see? Look around. Every couple walks side by side." I recall occasions where Mom would, perhaps unconsciously, drop back, and then Dad would stop and wait for her to catch up before walking again.

Mom and Grandma fought over Mom's westernized style of clothing. And they fought about Mom's lack of discipline in allowing my sisters to dress inappropriately for school.

Grandma would continue, "As long as we're talking about it, you shouldn't talk back to your husband. And why are you letting the girls eat the chicken drumsticks? You're supposed to save them for Lester! And you make him clear the table after meals?"

Mom was truly a feminist ahead of her time and culture. She would retort, "We're in modern America, Ma! We're not in the dark ages of China! Here in America, women matter as much as men and, furthermore, boys and girls get treated alike!

"You want me to be like Lee Moi?"

"Lee Moi deserved it," Grandma would argue. "She always talked back to her husband and even her father. Her husband finally had enough of her disrespect! She couldn't even bear him a boy!"

Lee Moi was legendary in Kee Hing Lee. She was pushed to her death off a footbridge by her husband for having a fourth daughter after numerous failed attempts to bring a boy into the family. The Chinese court convened and acquitted him on the basis of her excessive insubordination. This didactic legend was told many times to prenuptial girls, followed by the admonition, "Let this be a lesson to not talk back to your husband."

With the passage of the Hart-Celler Act, it was now much less complicated to bring everyone else over from Hong Kong. An immigration attorney would not even be necessary.

With all four stores providing abundant income, Mom and Dad decided they could bring everyone else to America at once after all. So, in advance, they paid the initial deposit and first month's rent on a three-bedroom house on 10th Street near Oakland Chinatown and bought one-way airfares for the seven of them.

For the sake of harmony, it was decided that Mom's mother would move in with Eddie (See Chew's newly adopted American name) and his family. Dad's mother would then live with us. It proved much more peaceful, as Dad's mother was much less opinionated and still performed many housekeeping chores for us.

Upon arrival, Uncle Eddie was necessarily and immediately hired by Dad. Dad required that Uncle Eddie learn English, so that he could eventually become a cashier. Mom took Kim to Oakland Chinatown to meet their friend who owned a sewing factory, so that she could go to work on the assembly line.

I remember Mom asking us to give up many of our various possessions as Uncle Eddie's family came here with very little. There were two boys and two girls. They were somewhat younger than we were, and we didn't mind giving up much of our clothing and shoes, which we had outgrown. We also gave up many of our toys and games as we were promised, and given, better replacements.

I remember Mom and Dad bought me a very enviable new Zenith transistor radio, so that I could give up my old Emerson.

Mom was glad that Dad bought her brand-new pots, pans, appliances, and some new furniture, so that Uncle Eddie's family could furnish their home with our old items. She was, of course, as pleased that Dad would take her to Capwell's Department Store and even the prestigious City of Paris Department Store in San Francisco to replenish her wardrobe after ceding her older clothing to her sister-in-law, Kim.

FRIDAYS WITH DAD

Fridays were special to me during my early grammar school years. Fridays, I had a difficult time paying attention to the teacher. "Lester! Pay attention! It's not Saturday yet!"

Miss Danielson was wrong. I wasn't looking forward to Saturday. I was looking forward to Dad picking me up right after school and taking me on his quality inspection rounds.

We would go from store to store, ranging from north Oakland, where he had a store on Adeline Street, all the way south to the Tennyson Road store in Hayward. At each store, he would chat with the managers, check inventory, look at ledger books, and probably do other stuff that was of little interest to me.

While these stops were painfully boring to me ("Dad, I'm tired. Can we go on to the next store?"), it was all the car rides in between that were special. It was our time together, just the two of us . . . no sisters. Our own special time.

When he wasn't talking to me, he enjoyed singing as he drove. Thinking back, he had an unusually deep baritone voice for a man his size. He would sometimes sing a Chinese song, which I could not follow. But, he also possessed a repertoire of American songs, mostly military . . .

"From the halls of Montezuma

To the shores of Tripoli,

We will fight our country's battles

On the land and on the sea . . ."

Eventually, I heard the "Marines' Hymn" enough to sing it along with him. We would go on . . .

"Off we go, into the wild blue yonder . . ."

Having sat at the table while Mr. Lau was tutoring Mom on the Constitution, I had learned much by osmosis. By the time I started school, I found that I could impress my teachers with all I knew about the U.S. government. But as important, I was very early on able to discuss politics with Dad. "Dad, are you a Republican or a Democrat?"

"I'm a businessman. Of course, I'm a Republican."

By the time it was dark on a full moon night during these Friday rounds, Dad would tell me to look out the windshield for the "man in the moon." As a child, I was never able to discern it. But to appease him, I pretended, "Oh yes, I see him." I never did find the image until recently. There was a full moon the second night after Dad died in 2013. Perhaps to validate my integrity with him, I searched for the man that night, and indeed the man in the moon finally revealed his face to me. I pretended it was Dad's face looking back down at me. Sometimes I still pretend so when it's a full moon night.

BUSINESS INSTINCT

I remember the entire family being awakened by a phone call around two o'clock one particular morning. Dad had to take off to see about an emergency at one of his stores. On most of these occasional middle of the night calls, a burglar alarm at one of his stores had been triggered. And most of those times, it would be a false alarm. So we all went back to bed.

But the next morning, it was different. Dad had not returned. Mom told us that there was a fire at store Number 4, and Dad had to stay out there. Then I remember before taking off for school seeing Dad being interviewed on TV news alongside two fire engines in front of this store at 14th and Peralta Streets. The façade of the building was completely charred, and the upper floor was completely gone. It was a disturbing sight. I felt like a child who had just seen an amputee for the first time. It was the one store where Mom and Dad owned the building.

It was later determined that construction equipment on the upper level created the voracious fire. The upper floor of this building had been empty apartments, empty and dilapidated through negligence even before Dad purchased it. It was Mom and Dad's ambition to renovate the upper floor into several living units that they could rent out. Unfortunately, the contractor had left a wallpaper steamer running through the night, which eventually vaporized all of its water and then ignited the wooden building.

Dad saw another opportunity here. With the insurance money, rather than trying to rebuild a similar structure with living quarters upstairs, he had a single-story cinder block building erected with three separate storefronts. Sav Mor Liquor Store Number 4 would occupy the larger corner space. Then, before construction even began, he had arranged a lease with a gentleman who wanted to operate a billiards room next to the store. Dad's business instinct was correct; he anticipated that the billiards room would significantly increase traffic into the liquor store. The third space was also already committed. Dad found a couple who very successfully operated a soul food kitchen there for many years.

I remember him commenting later that the increase in business in this store, because of the billiards room, was more than the rent he was collecting from the tenant.

A few years later, Dad met a friend who owned several successful self-service coin-operated laundries in the Bay Area. He offered to sell Dad one of his locations. Mom and Dad considered the offer seriously until Dad had an inspiration. "Sin, the parking lot behind Number 4 is never full. I think we can extend the building for a coin laundry and still park about a dozen cars. And the neighborhood is perfect. Most of the people in this area don't own their own washers and dryers, and there's not a coin laundry for at least a mile around us."

Thus, Sav Mor Launderette came to be and proved to be an avalanche of profit. Operating costs and maintenance were low, and volume was high. Especially on the weekends, none of all thirty washers and all ten dryers had any idle time. And again, just as Dad predicted with the billiards room, customers waiting for their wash added to the volume of business at the liquor store.

Mom would often smilingly remind him that it was she who insisted he buy the property along with the liquor business. Dad would simply grin at her in response. He knew she was right.

"ALLAN, I HAVE A RELATIVE IN CHINA"

Over time, word got around the Chinese community of what Allan and Sin Wong had done for Stanley and Eddie.

My sisters and I were often the beneficiaries of candy, cakes, and other gifts that people would bring to our home, so that they could have coffee with Mom and Dad. For a while at least, I thought these treats were their admission tickets to our home. As we got older, we realized these visits were from Chinese relatives (or friends who claimed kinship from the mere fact of having come from the same or nearby village in Canton) hoping that Dad would assist in the immigration of their own kin still in China or Hong Kong. Dad had the ability to guarantee employment.

The stories varied. A young Chinese American family missed the grandparents living in Hong Kong. A Chinese American man, Fung Quan, was having trouble bringing his recent bride back from China. (Even with the liberalization of immigration laws, the INS was always suspicious that recent marriages were shams.) A young couple, Lily and Jimmy, whose wife was the daughter of a very distant aunt of Mom's wanted to come to America to start their family with more opportunity and abundance—the very reason Dad first came here. Not all who came to Mom and Dad for help were Chinese.

A Caucasian friend (Tim) of a friend of Mom and Dad's wanted a Chinese bride. And Mom and Dad had a distant niece in China whom they felt would be a good match.

Obviously, Mom and Dad could not sponsor everyone. But I always knew who were the ones who "made the cut." They were the ones who were invited back numerous times for more coffee. In overhearing many of Mom and Dad's conversations after each of these people left, I surmised what the criteria were. Were the would-be immigrants hard working in China? Were they free of vices such as gambling or drinking? Did they show an interest in furthering their education here, particularly in learning English? Do they have or do they want to have children?

I remember often accompanying Mom and Dad to the San Francisco International Airport to pick up these new immigrants.

On many of these rides out to the airport, Dad would reminisce about the long steamer trips across the Pacific. "People are so lucky today. They get on an airplane, stop in Hawaii, and inside of one day they're already here."

But the more substantive conversations between Mom and Dad had to do with how they could help these people get started in America. "He knows how to drive. We'll help him get his license, so he can be a runner." (Merchandise often had to be moved from one store to another.) "He speaks some English. We'll try him out as a cashier. That will force him to improve." "She needs to go to night school to learn English since she'll be working in the daytime." "We'll need to take their children to get enrolled in school." "It's time to replace Jennie and Carolyn's beds. Let's give them the old ones." I was particularly pleased when Mom and Dad gave away my little thirteen-inch black-and-white RCA TV set and bought a nineteen-inch color Magnavox for my bedroom.

PAYING IT FORWARD

I don't think Uncle Art was even a remote uncle, but we children were told to address him so just out of respect. Uncle Art was probably a pretty good general manager of Dad's store on Adeline.

Dad had helped him and his wife immigrate here many years prior. We called his wife Auntie Goldfish because that was the literal translation of her Chinese name. She had assimilated so quickly that she was making cream puffs that would have pleased the de' Medici's (whose family chef created this incredible Italian indulgence centuries ago.) We as children always looked forward to visiting Auntie Goldfish as, perhaps out of gratefulness to my parents, she always had a batch of freshly made cream puffs waiting for us. (They were so light and angelically airy that I could eat three or four of them and report to Mom that I had eaten just one, although I never figured out how she had those proverbial eyes in the back of her head.)

During one of these visits, I remember Uncle Art telling Dad that an opportunity had come up for him to purchase a liquor store of his own near Berkeley. He was bold. Not only would he be leaving Dad's employ, but he told Dad he was about $5,000 short of making it happen and would like a loan.

Mom was adamantly opposed to this seemingly turncoat proposal. She and Dad argued much over this issue. Dad's position was, "I will always remember the people who helped me get started. Now it's my turn to be a benefactor. We can always find a new manager. But Art may never have this chance again. I've checked out the store, and it's a good deal. I would buy it myself, but I have more than enough to keep busy. I just want him to have the same chance I was given when I started."

In the end, Dad prevailed, took out his checkbook and wrote Uncle Art the check, and Art's Liquor became a reality. We children benefited from a guaranteed infinite stream of Auntie Goldfish's feathery light cream puffs. And eventually, Dad was repaid in full . . . the loan, that is, although he too was a big fan of her cream puffs.

Of course, in the same way that he was never charged interest on those handshake loans, Dad never received or expected interest payments whenever he loaned money out.

Beyond the reward of cream puffs, Uncle Art and Auntie Goldfish were known to spread the word through the Chinese community that the Gee's were such magnanimous and generous people. Dad was very philosophical about money matters. "Money is important, but your reputation is by far more important." Money is just a measuring stick. Reputation is the real currency of business.

Fung Quan, whom Dad had helped to overcome some immigration hurdles in order to bring his bride to America, wanted some financial help in buying into a restaurant partnership near the UC campus in Berkeley. But, rather than simply loaning Fung the shortage, Dad bought a silent partnership interest for the difference. Now Dad had more options for employing immigrants beyond the liquor retail business. He could hire busboys, dishwashers, and cooks. Uncle Eddie and Lily's husband, Jimmy, eventually had jobs at this restaurant. (I personally benefited from Dad's part ownership in Robbie's Hof Brau on Telegraph Avenue during my years at Berkeley. Anytime I, often with another college buddy, walked into the restaurant we would get a free meal.)

I remember that many of Mom's lectures on frugality included the virtue of her sewing our clothing. But, I was truly humbled to learn from Mom that Lily, sans machine, was making clothing by stitching seams together by hand, simply with needle and thread, for her three young children.

"Dad is getting me a new sewing machine, so that I can give my old Singer to them." Mom was excited that she would finally have a machine that could do zig-zag stitches, that could do stretch material, and that could power through denim. But I could tell that she was just as excited to be able to help Lily. "It must be very hard on her eyes and on her back to stitch everything by hand. Even though this old machine can only do straight stitches, she will really appreciate having a machine. I would hate to see her have eye or back problems in later life."

Her husband, Jimmy, was a hard worker. I would overhear Dad often comment to Mom, "Jimmy is a good employee. He's honest, he never complains, and he always keeps busy, even when there are no customers in the store. He will one day be a success." Through sheer hard work and thrift, this family eventually managed to amass enough to buy a dry cleaning business, which became successful beyond their expectations.

This business, in conjunction with grants and scholarships, enabled all three children—Leo, Alice, and Stella—to acquire not only bachelor's degrees, but post-graduate degrees from various Ivy League universities. Today, all three are professionals, each is married to a professional, and each couple has children. This family is exemplary of the consummate American dream . . . a true fulfillment of the promise of Gum Shan.

MY EDUCATION IN BUSINESS

My college education did not include a real MBA. But, I reflect back and realize that I had learned much more about business from shadowing Dad over the years than from all my years on college campuses. By the time I was in high school, I was already aware of and in awe of the street instinct Dad had in business. Today, I attribute much of my business sense to "the University of Allan Gee."

From the time I was in middle school, Dad would take me on "stakeouts." I always figured I was simply helping assuage his boredom as we would park across the street from a possible acquisition for what seemed like hours. I wasn't sure if he was actually talking to me or just muttering to himself while I was busy with a crossword puzzle or some books I had brought along to keep myself busy. But he would make comments out loud. "There have been only five customers in the last half hour. Only one of them walked out with a large bag and the other four probably had just a new pack of cigarettes in their pockets. Yesterday was payday. There should be much more business. It's not worth what they're asking." We wouldn't come back to this store. Then there was the one we staked out several different times and days on San Pablo Avenue. "Good traffic flow. They have a busy parking lot. There's traffic even the day before payday. Good price for a corner location. I think I'll make an offer." Thus, another Sav Mor Liquor Store. I was by osmosis learning marketing.

By the time I was in high school, every summer I had a job as a cashier behind the counter at Dad's Number 4 store in West Oakland. Sometimes, I had the privilege of working alongside Dad.

I recall one time when a customer had purchased a pint of Jim Beam bourbon that immediately escaped his grip as he was leaving. The shards of glass exploded through the brown paper bag and created a catastrophe of glass fragments and whiskey around a five-foot radius. Several boxes of Sunshine Saltine Crackers were drenched beyond salability.

"Aw, fuck! I'm so sorry! Gimme a mop, and I'll clean it up for you, Gee!"

Dad was his usual calm self. He actually laughed "Don't worry, Shorty. My son will clean it up. But come back here." Dad reached behind himself and grabbed another pint of Jim Beam from the shelf.

"Naw. I think I only have enough money left to get a half pint. Gimme a half pint, Gee."

"No, Shorty. You keep your money. You already paid me."

"Thank you, Gee. I'll pay you when I come back."

"No, Shorty. We're even Steven. OK?" Dad turned to me, "Son, get the mop and bucket."

While cleaning up, I told Dad, "You not only lost money on the whiskey, but you lost three boxes of crackers. Just look at these." I demonstrated by holding up a box by the corner as it still dripped Jim Beam.

"Only the boxes are damaged. Throw the boxes out. But the crackers are fine. Just rinse the wax bags, and we'll take them home for ourselves to eat.

"But no, I didn't lose any money, Son. It's like this. If I made him pay again for his whiskey, he might not come back here again. Remember, we have a competitor only three blocks from here. Not only that, he will probably tell others what a cheapskate I am. But, if I give up one pint of whiskey, plus three boxes of crackers by the way, he will keep coming back. The future profits will far more than make up for what I gave up today. It's something called 'goodwill.' Maybe you're too young to understand that yet."

Today I understand. If I make one customer happy, he might tell one other person. But, if I make one customer unhappy, he will go out and tell ten others. I had thus learned from Dad about PR [Public Relations, but Dad used to call it "Public Reputation," which seems somehow much more apt].

CAMELLIA PLACE

It would be Mom and Dad's last house, but that's because it was finally their dream house.

In the mid 1960s, we spent many weekends driving through the Oakland Hills, sometimes with and sometimes without a realtor. Mom had two primary criteria for a new home: It had to be large enough for entertaining and it had to have a view. Dad also had two, but very different, end goals: He wanted to sell the Athol house to Eddie for a token amount as his family had expanded to seven children by then. And second, more importantly—he told me this more than once—he would stop at nothing to make Mom happy. He shared with me the promise he made to himself on their wedding day back in Canton that he, starting out as a poor farm boy, would one day provide for Mom the life of luxury she had become accustomed to as a child.

Eventually, Mom saw what she liked . . . it was a partially completed two-level house on Camellia Place that the contractor waited to be sold before he would then finish the appointments to the buyer's wishes. And Mom had many wishes.

She hired a decorator to select the plush flooring, the silk and linen window coverings, and all new furniture. (Almost all our old furniture was left at the Athol house for Eddie's family.) Much of the new hand-crafted rosewood furniture was imported from China.

She had a restaurant-sized gas wok built into the kitchen counter. (Upon cooking in the wok for the first time, Mom and Dad realized that it required an industrial fan installed on the roof to adequately vent the entire house whenever the wok was in use, which was often.)

An opulent three-foot chandelier of shimmering Italian crystal hovered over a twelve-place dining table from a sixteen-foot high ceiling. This formal dining room had heard many years of clinking toasting flutes and clanging silverware. But most importantly, this room heard much conversation, sometimes arguments and, thankfully more often, hearty laughter. While for the traditional Chinese family, dinner was a somber time of contemplation and meditative quietness, our dinners often degenerated into raucous fits of laughter to the point of tears. Mom, particularly, not only laughed at, but often contributed to, the many off-color jokes when we were deemed old enough to laugh even about sex at the dinner table. Dad just grinned contently.

The walls were dressed with custom-framed artworks, mostly gathered from Mom and Dad's numerous travels and most of them depicting bucolic nature scenes, superannuated pagodas, or grand palaces. Almost all of them were hand-crafted in bright gossamer silk or almost photographic-detailed needlepoint, evidencing a combination of talent and skill over perhaps weeks, or even months, of pain.

The large cantilevered sundeck was furnished with beautifully crafted and tightly woven cane furniture. Often, as we sat out there, Mom would comment that she chose this furniture because it reminded her fondly of her father's cane furniture factory. But inevitably, she would break down in tears as she spoke of his demise. The pain never left her. And we children were always quick to offer a box of Kleenex.

The home was large (to accommodate all of us). It was spacious (for entertaining large parties). It was elegant (but in a quiet way). Yet it was never ostentatious. Exactly as Mom and Dad wanted their dream home.

They always appreciated comfort and high quality, but never for show. Nevertheless, the many guests who came for dinner or coffee spoke in high admiration of Mom and Dad's accomplishments. Nearly every Chinese guest who came by uttered the phrase, *"ho sai gai."* As with much of the Chinese language, there is not a precise and literal translation to convey the accurate sense of this phrase. But, it alludes to achieving a previously envisioned future of comfort and abundance. It is a high compliment.

In the Chinese culture, it is actually considered immodest to graciously accept a compliment such as this. In fact, it would be more appropriate to decline the compliment. Thus, Mom and Dad would verbally deny their own achievements. But in their hearts, they knew they had created *ho sai gai.*

Mom had a beautiful rhyming proverb that eloquently spoke of modesty. *"Dai fah heng, 'm hem guong yun teng."* Translated literally, it means "wearing a fragrant flower, you need not tell people."

The ultimate *pièce de résistance* of this home was the spectacular view—a magnificent sweeping view looking west. I often wondered what thoughts, what memories, and what emotions stirred in each of Mom and Dad as they gazed fixedly beyond the horizon over the entirety of the city of Oakland, beyond the shimmering silvery San Francisco Bay, above the San Francisco skyline, and across the majestic expanse of the Pacific Ocean, perhaps pretending they could see their Kee Hing Lee and Foo Shan villages in Toisan, Canton, from this palatial home perched high on the Oakland hillside . . . in America, Gum Shan.

THANKSGIVING

I suspect we violated the Oakland Fire Marshal's room capacities at our home every Thanksgiving. Mom and Dad invited every relative, friend, and store employee who did not have his or her own family to spend Thanksgiving with. Cars would be parked the entire length of the block on both sides of the street. Everyone took turns on a continual rotating basis to dine at one of several tables, on a sofa with a TV tray, or on a stool while precariously balancing a lap plate.

I was amazed that Mom, with the help of our two grand-mothers and a few of the guests, not only prepared the traditional American Thanksgiving menu with turkey, ham, stuffing, and sweet potato but also a full array of Chinese dishes, since many of the Chinese guests expected food more familiar to them. And then to produce all this in massive volumes that would rival a small restaurant! Sometimes two turkeys were roasted.

This voluminous production of food was so that as the satiated crowd started to thin out, Mom and Dad would create a seemingly endless assembly line of paper plates along the long kitchen counter, each plate heaped up high with the remaining food. Then each plate, neatly molded with a sheet of aluminum foil, would be loaded into Dad's car. Dad would set out to each store with these, so that his employees who were working that night could also enjoy the abundance of our kitchen.

By the time Dad returned, there was just our family. One time, as he sat down to finally reward himself with a slice of pumpkin pie, he espoused the meaning of Thanksgiving. "There's just no place like America."

A CHANCE REUNION AND THE NEXT GENERATION

The reunion took place in 1973 when I was away at graduate school. But the story had been told to me enough times that I sometimes think I was the proverbial fly on the wall, watching. Mom and Dad were at a wedding banquet somewhere in San Francisco. In the course of small talk with some people who shared a table with them, the conversation somehow meandered to their 1947 voyage aboard the USS *General W.H. Gordon* from China and Mom's experience in the infirmary. One of the persons at the table suddenly stood up and shrieked,

"You must be the same Gee Seen Sahng [a more formal way of saying Mr. Gee] that Gim Gnook talks about all the time! She remembers the two of you and speaks particularly of your kindness and caring when she was in the bed next to you on that ship. This is funny; she is here at this very dinner! I'll go bring her over."

They recognized each other instantly and the rest of the evening was spent catching up. Exchanging phone numbers, they promised to keep in touch.

Indeed, they did.

I was back visiting Mom and Dad (and my sister Emma who was still living at home at the time) for the Christmas holiday in 1974. Evidently, Gim Gnook, along with her youngest daughter, visited Mom a few times, and Emma became friends with the daughter. The first day I was back, Emma asked me to take her shopping in San Francisco. (Having just graduated from high school, she received her new car from Dad, as did each one of us, and she was reluctant to drive it across the Bay Bridge.)

"You don't mind if we stop and pick up a friend to go shopping, do you?"

"Anything for you, Emma. It's Christmastime."

It turned out that we were picking up Gim Gnook's daughter, Lila.

The following year, 1975, this very Lila and I were married.

A month after Bryce, our first of two sons, was born, Mom asked Lila to follow her to their bedroom. In the large walk-in closet, Mom pushed aside several Christian Dior dresses that cleverly hid a massive gray safe. As she deftly twirled the combination dial left and right alternately, she whispered to Lila, "I have something very special for you."

The dial clicked. She swung the squeaking heavy door open with some effort and a grunt, and the safe exhaled the smell of a bank lobby. She reached in and pulled out a small red velvet box, rattling it to confirm that it still held its contents. Unsnapping the brass clasp with a click, she pulled the lid back on its two brass hinges and extracted from a tangle of jewelry one polished but intricately carved deep-green stone piece set with a gold bail. "This jade pendant will bring the two of you good luck and wealth. It brought me good luck protecting our home when the Japanese invaded our village. I gave each one of my daughters something I was lucky enough to hide from the Japanese, but you too, Lila, are just like another daughter to me. So this is now yours."

She cupped the back of one of Lila's hands from underneath with her left hand and ceremoniously placed the jade firmly in Lila's palm, pressing down with her right hand. They embraced for a long time.

"I've waited a long time for this moment, Lila. My son is very lucky."

It was not until weeks later before Lila related this story to me and showed me the finely carved jade disk depicting two opposing fish suggesting the yin-yang symbol. Yin-yang signifies balance and harmony while fish symbolize abundance in Chinese culture. And, as Mom explained to Lila, fish also bring good luck and jade itself provides protective powers from physical danger.

DAD'S RETIREMENT

In 1984, when Dad turned sixty-five, he sold the last of his seven stores. Over a period of the five prior years, he had sold each store independently, holding onto his most profitable one, Store Number 4, until the end. This is the one store that today still bears the name "Sav Mor Liquors" at the corner of 14th and Peralta Streets. (Mom and Dad retained ownership of the property and continued to collect rental income on the four storefronts until 1995, when they decided that they no longer wanted the role of landlord and additionally recognized the eventual decline of real estate value in West Oakland. The building was sold to the then proprietor of the liquor store.)

Dad also recognized that with the repeal of the California fair trade laws, which had to his benefit dictated minimum retail pricing for liquor, it was a matter of time that the larger discounters (such as Liquor Barn and BevMo) would present difficult competition for his smaller chain. It was the right time to leave the liquor retail business.

It was a joyful retirement banquet as Dad recounted all that this business had meant to all of us. It bought a number of houses for us. It took us on many family vacations. It bought him a new luxury car nearly every two years. It bought each one of us children a new car as a reward upon graduating from high school. It put us children through some expensive colleges. And it was now going to enable Mom and Dad to travel the world.

But much more importantly, the business enabled him to empower many others to realize the American dream. At this celebration, he spoke fondly of the many families he had sponsored. He spoke gleamingly of the at least fifty immigrants and their children that he and Mom empowered from humble beginnings to ultimate success, many of whom were at this celebratory banquet. When Mom spoke proudly of the many children graduating from prestigious universities (including Harvard, Yale, UC Berkeley, and Stanford), she spoke beamingly as if they were her own children graduating.

Dad reminded us that his childhood started out gathering pig dung for fertilizer in China. He spoke of coming to America with a mere trunk of clothing and fifty dollars. He spoke of their seven-year separation during the war. He did not forget to acknowledge all his benefactors—his sponsor Uncle Som, his welcoming cousins Lily, Flora, and Quong, his first employer Mr. Lee, and Teddy who gave him the first opportunity to start his own business.

BACK TO THE VILLAGE

During Dad's working years, Mom and Dad's travels were mostly restricted to the United States and Canada and usually for no more than a week at a time. But once retired and unfettered, they traveled internationally nearly every year until Mom's health began failing in the mid 1990s. We could vicariously follow their numerous travels by the multitude of stamps in their passports.

They had traveled mostly to Asia, including Hong Kong, China, Singapore, Thailand, and Malaysia. And on some trips they were now able to be gone for more than two months. While they usually joined luxury tour groups, there were a few trips to Guangdong (formerly Canton) that they took on their own to see their motherland.

Mom and Dad did discover that the large city centers, such as the capital city of Guangzhou, had become metropolized and very modern with light-rail systems, department stores, and even KFCs. But things in the rural areas where they had grown up hadn't changed much over the forty or so years since they left. The same primitive earthen buildings with the crude wooden doors and hard sandstone floors still served as homes. The inhabitants still worked the rice fields with ox-drawn single-share plows. Toileting was still done in a communal building with a mere hole in the floor of each of several walled-off stalls. A few of the wealthier residents did acquire piped-in water, telephones, electricity, and even television.

The main road leading to the village gate was now paved so that motor scooters and bicycles replaced the rickshaws and ox-drawn carts. But these newer conveyances were still hauling the same rice, chicken, and vegetables into town. The six-story watchtower at the gate, which now faintly announced "Kee Hing Lee," had been neglected into shambles from disuse. It had at one time served to protect the village from warlords and marauders and finally from the Japanese during World War II (although that was to no avail).

The edifice that Dad was born in and first knew as home had suffered the same forlorn fate as the watchtower. It had been unoccupied for decades save for some rodents.

On their subsequent trips back to Kee Hing Lee, Mom and Dad went prepared to offer what financial help they could. On one particular trip, they helped fund a badly needed hospital building. On another trip, they helped with a new school building.

Although they no longer had relatives in their respective villages, their names were recognized and they were elevated to royalty level when they visited.

After many of their excursions, Mom and Dad were always excited to share with us pictures and stories of the experiences, the scenery, and the new friends they had made. But far more remarkable were their stories of visits to their homeland. Mom spoke in her usual compassionate way of how difficult life still was for the people in the farming villages. Dad would utter, "If only they all had the same opportunities we in America have."

MOM, FEBRUARY 10, 1922– NOVEMBER 11, 1997

Mom must have had a tremendous physical constitution. She had survived three medical episodes over her last fifteen or so years of life: two heart attacks and a stroke. She even fully recovered from her stroke although she would never dare to drive again.

The phone call from Dad was an inevitable. But no one could have predicted when it would come. She succumbed to a massive heart attack in their bedroom on November 11, 1997, at the age of seventy-five. Dad's voice was his predictable-but-unique calm. "Mommy is gone. They came with loud sirens, but they took her away in the ambulance quietly. Can you come up and stay with me tonight?" Lila and I stayed the next two months with him.

It was a standing-room-only funeral. The anthill of mourners spilled out into the hallway of the chapel. Many came to not just mourn or say "goodbye," but to say, "thank you" to her. To thank her for her limitless generosity. For her deep compassion for those less fortunate. For her endurance and sacrifices.

I had the honor of delivering the closing comment. Just days before the service, the words spontaneously came to me in the form of a poem with very little effort:

Mother Sun

She toils and struggles the morning Sun
And labors to Her glory of noon.
She pauses, reserved of strength and might
Effusing Her infinite benevolence and light.

Her inexhaustible generosity flows
Forever changing those who allow.
Enriching all within her keep;
But now She's tired; it's time to sleep.

And thus, the giving day is done
As She retires 'neath the horizon.
In morn we'll immortalize Her gifts
Too many, too large for an epitaph.

WIDOWHOOD

Lila and I commuted between Oakland and our office in San Jose for two months. But the arduous one-and-one-half, sometimes two-hour morning drive on the 880 freeway became a privilege. Although Dad said he was fine alone in the daytime, we worked only in the mornings and returned to him by early afternoon.

"I'm okay by myself in the daytime. But it's very lonely at night. I wish I had never complained so much to her about her loud snoring. How I now wish I could be disturbed in the middle of the night by that snoring again.

"Next year we would have been married sixty-one years. Imagine, sixty years. We actually have two wedding dates, you know? I married her again under American law after the war.

"We were talking about another vacation to China. She wanted to see her Foo Shan village home just one more time.

"And now I have no one to cook for anymore.

"Lila, would you move her clothes out into the hall closet? It's too hard for me to see them when I get dressed in the morning."

For all my childhood years when Dad was my Superman, my protector, it was now my turn to give back consolation and comfort. For the time I was frightened by thunder, for the time he used the garden hose to beat away a dog that attacked me while he was washing his car, and for the time he bought me ice cream when he accidentally closed the car door before my foot was inside . . . it was now my turn.

I gleaned one thing from watching Dad in widowhood: I do not want to predecease Lila. I love her too much to imagine her having to endure the tortuous agony of widowhood. When the time comes, it would be best that we each go within moments of the other. If not, let me be the one to grieve, not Lila.

ELAINE

In December of 1998, Allan wrote the following letter to the INS and attached a visa application along with an Affidavit of Support on behalf of He Xiao Ling ("Elaine" was her American name.) This is the letter verbatim:

To whom it may concern:

My name is Allan Gee. I am a U.S. citizen and a veteran. I am recently retired. My wife passed away on 11/11/1997. I have been very lonely and sad since then.

I have an old friend named Dick Fong whom I have known for years. He cares about me and understands how I felt after I lost my wife. He mentioned about a friend of his named He Xiao Ling who is 56 years old and had never been married before. Dick asked me if I was interested in being introduced to her. I started to phone her and communicated by letters in January of 1998. Months later, we wanted to meet each other in person.

On 11/9/1998, I went to China to visit Xiao Ling with my daughter Emma and her two children. I found Xiao Ling to be a wonderful person. She arranged everything for us from where to stay to the tour itinerary. She took care of me during the whole trip and made me feel warm and loved. She did foot massages for me. She was also concerned about my health and diet. She reminded me to drink milk and have a warm bath before going to bed so I could sleep better. The other reason I love Xiao Ling is that she loves her 85 year old mother and takes care of her.

After coming back from China, I continued to maintain communication with her. I have made a lot of long distance phone calls to her. We talk on the phone for more than 15 minutes each time and we have a lot to tell each other. Since I met her, my life has been changed. I need her care and love. She told me she loves me because I am a good hearted man. She has become the most

*important person in my life. If I have not received a letter within
10 days, I would call her right away. Ever since we have known
each other, I have received more than 30 letters from Xiao Ling.*

*As I am getting older, I need a woman I love who can understand
me and care about me. My fiancée, Xiao Ling, loves me too. We
both hope we can spend the rest of our lives together and enjoy
our retired lives. I sincerely hope that you can approve her visa
application so she can come to the U.S. to marry me.*

Thank you very much for your consideration.

Sincerely yours,

Allan Gee

In less than a month, his petition was approved.

Elaine more than lived up to everyone's hopes and expectations for Dad. She was a kind and thoughtful person not just
to Dad, but to everyone else in the family. She gave Dad eleven
years of attentiveness that never wavered. And she always welcomed every one of us in the family with a warm and sincere
smile. She was an optimist and her positivity was indomitable
as proven in her final days.

Elaine quickly assumed nearly all the shared responsibili-
ties that we children and some of the grandchildren had borne
after Mom's death. We had taken him to doctor's appointments,
made sure he was eating properly, and mollified his loneliness.

But most importantly, Elaine rekindled Dad's spirit and
soul. Like adding a seasoned dry eucalyptus log to an almost
extinguished hearth, the cool and lazily pulsating embers all
at once burst into a vigorous, blinding, and energetic dancing
conflagration again.

Dad renewed his interest and active participation in the Gee
Family Association, a family fraternal organization that bene-
fits local charities such as the Chinatown Children's Hospital in

San Francisco, where children can be treated at no cost to the parents. He had previously been actively committed to the organization's causes, having served two separate terms as president of the San Francisco Chapter before Mom died. Afterwards, he gradually lost interest in participating even as a member. Now reinvigorated, he was warmly welcomed back. Knowing that Elaine was the catalyst, everyone there also embraced his new wife. The rest of us in the family witnessed this as we once again attended the annual association banquets.

The piano that resided dormant in Dad's living room had neither been tuned nor even played by anyone in years. On one of my visits, as I approached the front porch, I recognized a piano tune emanating from inside that I remembered hearing Dad play when I was a mere child. After several pokes on the doorbell button went ignored, I bruised my knuckle rapping on the iron gate. Abruptly the music stopped, and the thudding of footsteps neared. Elaine appeared as the door swung open with Dad standing right behind her.

"Who was that playing the piano?"

"Your father. He's very talented! I had no idea, and I'm really enjoying it."

Family events, including birthdays, Christmas, Thanksgiving, and Chinese New Year were special once again. Elaine never forgot each grandchild's birthday; there was again always a generously cash-filled red envelope each time. And, it was remarkable and touching that she referred to each family member as "my" grandchild, "my" daughter, "my" son. And everyone felt so natural in assuming these mantles.

Eventually, Dad wanted Elaine to learn English. Dad would drop her off at the very same Chinese Community Center where Mom had learned English more than fifty years ago. And in due time, she acquired a quite functional fluency with conversational English.

At some point, her proficiency moved to reading comprehension such that she was able to take and pass the California driver's license written exam. Of course, Dad enrolled her in driving school and thenceforth purchased a new Toyota Camry for her.

That it was a Toyota was somewhat a breakthrough for Dad. He had often while Mom was still alive contemplated the economic wisdom of purchasing a Japanese car. But any such suggestion from Dad was always immediately arrested by Mom's vivid and tearful recollection of her father's demise in the hands of the Japanese during the war.

Elaine's abilities with driving and the English language were possibly the result of benevolence or good forethought (or both) on Dad's part. As his physical and mental capacities began to wane in his later years, Elaine's caring nature became even more evident as she would drive him to doctor's appointments, drive him to association and family functions, and pick up groceries and medication.

ULTIMATE VALOR

There was perhaps no stronger testimony to Elaine's devotion to Dad than her resolve to shield Dad from emotional distress.

In September 2011, Elaine was taken to the emergency room of Alta Bates Hospital in Berkeley, complaining of severe dizziness and overall disorientation. The family was completely astonished to learn that she had been combating cancer for more than three years in complete secrecy.

In the privacy of the hospital room that September, Elaine revealed to Lila that she had kept silent on her suffering lest any family member might inadvertently divulge the stressful news to Dad, recognizing that Dad himself was physically and mentally ailing.

As Lila learned in that conversation, Elaine had been diagnosed with lung cancer three years prior. She had been driving herself to chemotherapy and radiation treatments on her own but telling Dad that she was grocery shopping, going to the bank, or engaging in some other mundane chore. Ultimately, she was in remission for nearly a year after which time the cancer returned and metastasized relentlessly. But again, in her pains to maintain secrecy, she continued to drive herself to her treatments . . . and when she could no longer drive without a struggle, she would take the bus!

Yet, throughout these incredible challenges, she had continued to partake in what had become the usual family functions. She never stopped smiling in front of us. She continued querying about everyone's wellness. She still never forgot a birthday.

And she never lost her sense of humor. After she revealed all her struggles to Lila, she let out a robust laugh and declared, "I was a good actress, wasn't I? I deserve an award, don't I?"

Ultimate valor is not what you endure for your own benefit, but what you endure for the sake of someone else.

We had the gift of having had Elaine still with us for about five more weeks, during which time we were all able to let her know how much she was appreciated, respected, and loved.

And although Dad was no longer capable of articulating his own thoughts, we made sure she knew that it was she who had helped Dad revert to the vibrant, active, and giving person he had always been before Mom died. She was the catalyst who touched the unsightly dormant gray cocoon of spooled gossamer filaments and triggered his metamorphosis into the lively, magnificent, and princely monarch butterfly.

We made sure she knew how much all of us, especially Dad, appreciated the pure and unconditional devotion she had given to all of us, even when confronted with seemingly insurmountable health challenges.

She had selflessly bestowed upon Dad, and the rest of us, some of the best years of our lives.

And she reciprocated in kind. She thanked all of us for having received her so warmly when she first arrived. She admitted to initially having had apprehensions that we might not have accepted her as a new family member. Of course, that fear was quickly proven unwarranted. And she expressed her greatest gratification for the life Dad had given her. Not only had he pampered her with the comforts and luxuries she only dreamt of when she lived in China, but he had given her his usual kindness and caring everyone knew him for. We did not know, although we were certainly not surprised to learn from her deathbed, that he had been giving her money monthly to send back to her mother in Guangzhou the entire time they were married. (Later we found the eleven years of monthly Western Union Moneygram receipts.)

We were comforted with knowing that on November 8, 2011, Elaine died knowing how we all felt about her.

"Ignorance is bliss" would be an apt cliché at this point. In the last year of Dad's life with dementia, he had virtually no awareness of Elaine's presence or absence. Sitting next to me at Elaine's memorial service, Dad pointed to the sixteen-by-twenty-inch black-and-white photo of Elaine up at the altar and said to me, "That's the tenant who rents a room in my house. Did she pay her rent for this month?"

Therein was the silver lining in the cloud. Dad did not have to endure the grief of a second widowhood.

Her ashes were shipped back to Guongzhou as she had wished. Her one-hundred-year-old mother was still alive there. While Dad had a legal claim to a pension fund Elaine had accrued as a pharmacist in China because of their years of marriage, my siblings and I were certain that Dad would have ceded it to her own family. Under Power of Attorney, we unanimously agreed to and executed a quit claim to the funds, so that her family would have it.

EDDIE AND ADA

I would be remiss if I failed to mention an extraordinary husband and wife couple, both of whom were the professional in-home caregivers for Dad and Elaine, and ultimately in Dad's final two years of life.

As Dad's Parkinson's disease advanced and the resulting dementia began to set in, we (my sisters and I) tried out a number of caregivers. They were mostly very competent and dependable. But each of them carried an air of sterility as they performed their duties in almost clinical fashion. Feeling that something more visceral was desired and missing, we continued trying different caregivers . . .

Until we met Eddie and Ada. This couple, in their forties, exemplified a rare marriage in that they worked together in the same job, harmoniously showing a unique combination of patience and temperament. This spoke highly of their innate capacity for caring and consideration for each other. And this compassion extended to everyone they encountered, particularly to Dad.

It didn't take long for us to notice that they had virtually "adopted" Dad and Elaine as if they were a part of their own family. (And today, we regard Eddie and Ada as part of our own family as we continue to include them in our family functions as much as possible.)

Since we hired Eddie and Ada when Elaine was last hospitalized, Elaine had the benefit of their care for about five weeks before she died.

Eddie and Ada not only performed the routine chores of cooking, cleaning, bathing, medicating, etc. for Dad. Several times a week, they would take him out, an awkward task maneuvering an unwieldy wheelchair and a heavy and bulky walker specially designed for Parkinson's patients. They would take him to Lake Merritt where he could feed the ducks and geese. They would take him to Chinatown for dim sum (assorted Chinese dumplings served with tea). Or they would simply take him out for a walk in the neighborhood.

Eventually, I realized that he was more cooperative with them than with me. (Every Monday afternoon, I would relieve them and spend the night at Dad's home.) I certainly did not take personal offense to this; I was very pleased that he had such a good relationship with his caregivers. "Are you going to drive me home? You didn't do my diaper right, Lester. Take me home, so that the young man [Eddie] there can do it." (He was, of course, already home, just confused.)

Eddie and Ada understood something about "quality of life" that most of us speak of but so narrow-mindedly take at face value. Most of us think of quality of life as still possessing all our faculties and abilities. "If he can't hear anymore, he no longer has quality of life." "If she can't travel anymore, she no longer has quality of life." "If he can't read and comprehend a story anymore, he no longer has quality of life." Thus, we tend to judge quality of life only with respect to our own realm, parameterized by our own awareness of expectations.

One day, Eddie and Ada brought to my attention that there were two things that Dad responded to most, two things that still made him "smile," as Eddie characterized it. When Eddie pointed out those moments to me, I realized what Eddie was calling a "smile" was that familiar look of unspoken contentment I had seen on Dad's face so many times in all his proudest moments. It was not a teeth-baring smile, but a calm grin. His head would tilt slightly higher than normal. His eyes would be almost half closed. I saw it the day Lila and I got married. I saw it when he held his first grandson, Ryan (son of Jennie). I saw it whenever we were all gathered around the dinner table for our Christmas dinner, for a family member's birthday, or just to get together. (It must have been the same appearance as he gazed at me through that Cyclone fence in the schoolyard on my first day of kindergarten.)

The two things Eddie referred to that brought on that special countenance were being surrounded by his family members and the good taste of food.

Exactly a week before Dad's death, we held a dim sum lunch at one of Dad's favorite restaurants on the Emeryville Marina. About a dozen of us, including Eddie and Ada of course, were able to make it.

While he addressed each of us by some other family member's name, he beamed that familiar look of contentment, knowing that we were there. He had forgotten that Mom had died sixteen years ago and asked, "Why isn't Mom here yet? She must be in heavy traffic." Regardless, it was apparent he was happy to see the many of us. He scanned the table and continued with that face of contentment.

By that final week, Dad had lost the muscles for swallowing. When the various dishes were brought to the table, Eddie would break off and place a small piece of *har gow* (shrimp dumpling) or pork bun *(char shui bow)* filling in his mouth. Dad would chew slowly extracting all the flavor from that morsel. That look of contentment again emanated from his face. Once all the flavor had been expended, Eddie would place a cupped hand under Dad's chin, and he knew to spit out the exhausted remnant. This would continue through the entire meal.

In the realm of Dad's world, with no awareness of what he could no longer do, he was content. He was surrounded by family and he was enjoying the good taste of his favorite food. Indeed, he perceived a quality of life within his own frame of reference. He thus surely had quality of life to the very end.

FINAL PASSAGE

It was February 15, 2013, in a small conference room of the emergency room at Alta Bates Hospital with the doctor on duty, Emma, and me. Dad was unresponsive that morning, so we had an ambulance bring him in. Although I had already anticipated what the answer would be, perhaps out of wishful thinking I ventured to ask the doctor about the possibility of Dad surviving to witness each of our two sons' weddings, Bryce's in April and Brent's in July of that year.

She was blunt. "Your father has less than a week. We're going to check him into a private room, and I'll arrange for unlimited family visits twenty-four hours, but he won't be leaving here alive. You should inform all of your family members. He is in hospice mode."

Most of us were already there at the hospital, but over the week more family members showed up and we wanted to be sure that there would never be a moment that he would be alone. We did not want him to be unaccompanied in his final moment.

Dad would lapse in and out of consciousness. And, in his conscious moments, he had varying degrees of lucidity.

We always had music in the room. Music had always been an important part of his life, and many of his progeny inherited his musical genes. Musical talent was particularly manifest in grandchildren David, Nicole, and Bryce.

He responded to "Butterfly Lover's Concerto" by moving his toes in rhythm as if to tap. In China, the butterfly symbolizes fresh and frolicsome love. Appropriately, he also responded by opening his eyes to "O Mio Babino Caro," a beautiful aria from Puccini's opera *Gianni Schicchi* where a girl sings praises of her father after his death. The title of the aria translates to "Oh, my beloved father."

He opened his eyes and correctly identified and addressed Lila at one point.

Our sons shared the final, and one of the finest, of Dad's moments of cognizance. Each of Bryce and Brent had brought their respective fiancées, Jennifer and Lena, with them. When our sons informed Dad that they were each getting married soon, Dad opened his eyes and addressed the girls, "You can go ahead and call me 'Grandpa' now." And they each did so.

Upon being shown the sapphire engagement rings (both girls preferred sapphire,) Dad's predictably traditional mindset came to play. "Why no diamonds?"

Both Bryce and Brent were quick to respond almost in unison, "I got her what would make her happy." Dad had spent his entire married life trying to make Mom, and then Elaine, happy. And that was Dad's last moment of actual consciousness. It was then okay with me that Dad could not be physically present at each of their weddings.

On February 22, not knowing that it would be Dad's final day, a number of us were discussing who would go to dinner and who would stay with him. Most of us had not eaten the entire day. Then Eddie and Ada offered to watch, so that all of the rest of us could go out. We each took turns telling Dad we would be back after dinner, although no one was sure if he comprehended. And we all left with an unspoken concern that he would be gone by the time we would return. Interestingly and knowingly, we ate (very rapidly) at the venue where Brent and Lena would be hosting their wedding.

Upon our return, we all immediately focused on the bedding over Dad's chest. The sheet was still rising and falling, rising and then falling, but noticeably more feebly than before we left for dinner. Surrounding his bed, every pair of eyes intently watched and every set of ears listened as his breaths become shallower and shallower and farther in between. All ears tuned into his soft rasping in the otherwise dead silence of the room. Then like a departing train whistling away into a distant camp, his breathing faded until it was suddenly imperceptible. He had waited for us before drawing his final breath.

It was on a workday that we held Dad's funeral. It is sometimes said that the final judge of esteem and respect for a deceased is measured by attendance at the funeral on a workday. The swarm of people overflowed into the hallway of the chapel. It was SRO—Standing Room Only. And amidst the congestion of mourners, the many (and some very large) bouquets and wreaths crowded and spilled like an overfilled dam from each side of the aisles out into the hallway.

As the only son, I was privileged to receive the American flag after he was given military honors and Taps were played at his graveside.

And thus, his odyssey in pursuit of *ho sai gai* came to full fruition and closure. Nay, not closure, continuity. Mom and Dad had exemplified for us immortality through deeds, and I now fully embrace the message of the Dalai Lama: One small pebble, a thousand ripples. It now becomes our charge to perpetuate Mom and Dad's altruistic spirits beyond future generations.

A VIEW OF MOTHERLAND

As I reflect on all that has gone into this book, I no longer wonder what thoughts, what memories, and what emotions stir up in each of Mom and Dad as their side-by-side resting place has them facing west overlooking the entire city of Oakland, beyond the shimmering silvery San Francisco Bay, above the San Francisco skyline, and across the majestic expanse of the Pacific Ocean. They could now forever see their Kee Hing Lee and Foo Shan villages in Toisan, Canton, from the lofty Oakland hillside . . . in America, Gum Shan—the Golden Mountain.

Farewell. 2013.

EPILOGUE

Sylvia (So Jing) and her husband, Stanley, are retired. Their daughter, Nancy, is married to Jimmy, a Silicon Valley engineer, and they are raising three children, Christopher, Gemma, and Esme.

Jennie, who succumbed to breast cancer at the premature age of forty-two, left us her son, Ryan, from Arnold. Ryan, who is a Silicon Valley engineer, is married to Wei Wei, and they are raising a daughter, Adelyn, and a son, Caden.

Carolyn and Raleigh, married forty-three years, are happily retired in Honolulu, having been an accomplished graphic artist and a Lockheed engineer, respectively.

I and my wife, Lila, married forty-two years, have two sons. Bryce, a law partner, is married to Jennifer, also an attorney, and they are raising their daughter, Avery. Brent, who has an MBA, is in the finance department of a large and successful concern and is married to Lena, who also has an MBA. They are raising their two sons, Harrison and Nolan.

Edna exemplifies for us a true survivor. Despite her life-long struggles with functional Down Syndrome, her spirit for kindness and generosity never has and never will be broken. Widowed several years ago, she is spreading her joy, living in a senior facility.

Emma, widowed while her two children from Joel were very young, accomplished the near impossible on her own.

While advancing herself through various career positions and adding numerous advanced degrees along the way, culminating in a recent PhD, she singlehandedly raised Nicole, who will be receiving her MD soon, and David who inherited his grandfather's musical talent and is a professional conductor. Nicole recently married Dave, who possesses a PhD in physics and is pursuing a law degree. Today, Emma and Wes share a beautiful view home in Berkeley, California.

ACKNOWLEDGMENTS

M y most sincere gratitude to all who played a role in my writing endeavor:

My wife, my now forty-three-year soulmate, Lila, who has always been unquestioningly supportive of all my pursuits. Over the last six years, she with her constant side-by-side encouragement and cheering, did more than anyone else to shape this book. Additionally, her vast knowledge of Chinese culture made this book more accurate and, by the way, made me a "better Chinese." Her steel-trap memory provided numerous anecdotes depicted in this book.

My sister, Emma Gordon, who provided much time, energy, and effort critiquing and discussing the manuscript in addition to furnishing numerous of the photographs included in this book.

My editor, my mentor, Dean Burrell, who continually gave me objective and constructive feedback and who dedicated countless hours to making this book a reality, right down to the technical aspects.

My informal "Board of Lay Editors" who critiqued my many iterations of the manuscript from a friend's perspective, who took time to discuss various personal and philosophical aspects of the story: Thomas Beck, Thomas Kanaley, Phillip Quigley, Tracy Quinton.